T4-AFY-031

NEW DIRECTIONS FOR EVALUATION
A PUBLICATION OF THE AMERICAN EVALUATION ASSOCIATION

Gary T. Henry, *Georgia State University*
COEDITOR-IN-CHIEF

Jennifer C. Greene, *University of Illinois*
COEDITOR-IN-CHIEF

Responding to Sponsors and Stakeholders in Complex Evaluation Environments

Rakesh Mohan
Washington State Joint Legislative Audit and Review Committee

David J. Bernstein
Montgomery County, Maryland, Department of Finance

Maria D. Whitsett
Austin Independent School District

EDITORS

Number 95, Fall 2002

JOSSEY-BASS
San Francisco

#5071049

RESPONDING TO SPONSORS AND STAKEHOLDERS IN COMPLEX EVALUATION
ENVIRONMENTS
Rakesh Mohan, David J. Bernstein, Maria D. Whitsett (eds.)
New Directions for Evaluation, no. 95
Jennifer C. Greene, Gary T. Henry, Coeditors-in-Chief

Microfilm copies of issues and articles are available in 16mm and 35mm,
as well as microfiche in 105mm, through University Microfilms Inc., 300
North Zeeb Road, Ann Arbor, Michigan 48106-1346.

New Directions for Evaluation is indexed in Contents Pages in Education,
Higher Education Abstracts, and Sociological Abstracts.

Print ISSN: 1097-6736; Online ISSN: 1534-875X ISBN: 0-7879-6346-1

NEW DIRECTIONS FOR EVALUATION is part of The Jossey-Bass Education
Series and is published quarterly by Wiley Subscription Services, Inc., A
Wiley Company, at Jossey-Bass, 989 Market Street, San Francisco, Cali-
fornia 94103-1741.

SUBSCRIPTIONS cost $69.00 for U.S./Canada/Mexico; $93 international. For
institutions, agencies, and libraries, $145 U.S.; $185 Canada; $219 inter-
national. Prices subject to change.

EDITORIAL CORRESPONDENCE should be addressed to the Editors-in-Chief,
Jennifer C. Greene, Department of Educational Psychology, University of
Illinois, 260E Education Building, 1310 South Sixth Street, Champaign,
IL 61820, or Gary T. Henry, School of Policy Studies, Georgia State Uni-
versity, P.O. Box 4039, Atlanta, GA 30302-4039.

www.josseybass.com

Printed in the United States of America on acid-free recycled paper con-
taining at least 20 percent postconsumer waste.

Editorial Policy and Procedures

New Directions for Evaluation, a quarterly sourcebook, is an official publication of the American Evaluation Association. The journal publishes empirical, methodological, and theoretical works on all aspects of evaluation. A reflective approach to evaluation is an essential strand to be woven through every volume. The editors encourage volumes that have one of three foci: (1) craft volumes that present approaches, methods, or techniques that can be applied in evaluation practice, such as the use of templates, case studies, or survey research; (2) professional issue volumes that present issues of import for the field of evaluation, such as utilization of evaluation or locus of evaluation capacity; (3) societal issue volumes that draw out the implications of intellectual, social, or cultural developments for the field of evaluation, such as the women's movement, communitarianism, or multiculturalism. A wide range of substantive domains is appropriate for *New Directions for Evaluation;* however, the domains must be of interest to a large audience within the field of evaluation. We encourage a diversity of perspectives and experiences within each volume, as well as creative bridges between evaluation and other sectors of our collective lives.

The editors do not consider or publish unsolicited single manuscripts. Each issue of the journal is devoted to a single topic, with contributions solicited, organized, reviewed, and edited by a guest editor. Issues may take any of several forms, such as a series of related chapters, a debate, or a long article followed by brief critical commentaries. In all cases, the proposals must follow a specific format, which can be obtained from the editor-in-chief. These proposals are sent to members of the editorial board and to relevant substantive experts for peer review. The process may result in acceptance, a recommendation to revise and resubmit, or rejection. However, the editors are committed to working constructively with potential guest editors to help them develop acceptable proposals.

Jennifer C. Greene, Coeditor-in-Chief
Department of Educational Psychology
University of Illinois
260E Education Building
1310 South Sixth Street
Champaign, IL 61820
e-mail:jcgreene@uiuc.edu

Gary T. Henry, Coeditor-in-Chief
School of Policy Studies
Georgia State University
P.O. Box 4039
Atlanta, GA 30302-4039
e-mail: gthenry@gsu.edu

CONTENTS

EDITORS' NOTES

The chapters in this volume explore the hard realities increasingly faced by evaluation practitioners today.[1] Evaluators must supply services that meet a broad array of stated and sometimes unstated needs, many of which are inherently social and political. Evaluators must address an increased demand for more services in fiscally constrained environments where "overhead" and "administrative activities" have a hard time competing with the provision of direct services. Further, given the variety of evaluation sponsors (authorities or clients who pay for an evaluation or employ the evaluator) and stakeholders (parties, including program clients who may be affected by evaluation processes and results), evaluators may find themselves in a bit of quandary when responding to the question, "For whom are we doing this evaluation anyway?"

One gauge of success of an evaluation is sponsors' and stakeholders' use of the knowledge gained from it, with the hope that evaluation use will lead to a social good of some kind. Most successful evaluators can provide timely, compelling, readily understood, fair, and useful knowledge to key players (sponsors and stakeholders). To the extent that the success of an evaluation is contingent on its use by sponsors and stakeholders, it becomes necessary to understand the authorizing sociopolitical environment in which evaluators operate, which will be referred to in this volume as the "evaluation authorizing environment" or "authorizing environment."

The authorizing environment is the situational and practical context within which evaluations are funded and expectations are set for evaluative activities, products, and use of evaluation results. The authorizing environment can be characterized along several dimensions, including formality, complexity, and the degree to which evaluative information is needed. The authorizing environment includes explicit stakeholders, namely the agency or elected body that initiates, authorizes, or sponsors an evaluation, as well as the agencies that operate the programs or services being evaluated. The authorizing environment also includes implicit stakeholders, including program staff, service recipients, community members, interest groups, and others who may have little control over the initiation of an evaluation but who, as we shall see in several of the chapters that follow, have a great deal of control over the process of planning and conducting an evaluation; in extreme cases, they may control whether an evaluation can be conducted

We would like to express our sincere thanks to Gary Henry, coeditor-in-chief of *New Directions for Evaluation*. Without Gary's support and encouragement, this volume would not have been possible. During the review process, he offered valuable suggestions that helped us improve the quality of the manuscript.

effectively. The relationships contained within the authorizing environment among various stakeholders are as important as the particular individuals or entities, because these relationships can also influence the funding, planning, conduct, use, and acceptance of the evaluation.

Authorizing environments of state and local government evaluators are further complicated by two key factors: (1) state and local government evaluations affect the way public policies are formulated and funds are used, and (2) the potential interplay of three levels of government—federal, state, and local—includes the coexisting and functioning of differently sized government bureaucracies and the delicate issues of federal versus state versus local rights and responsibilities.

The importance of understanding these multifaceted relationships is captured to some extent in the American Evaluation Association's (AEA) Guiding Principles for Evaluators (American Evaluation Association, 1995), particularly Principle Five, which describes evaluators' responsibilities for general and public welfare. This guiding principle requires evaluators to consider the diverse values and interests of all stakeholders and to consider those values and interests along with the needs of the evaluation client. Existing literature accepts the criticality of politics in the practice of evaluation, as discussed in Chelimsky's seminal article titled "The Politics of Program Evaluation" (1987). Palumbo (1987) graphically represents the distinctions between developmental cycles for information and policymaking but does not clearly delineate the dynamics between the two or determine when or if they interact. Even the conceptual framework presented by Lester and Wilds (1990) for understanding knowledge utilization does not fully address the layers of complexity introduced by consideration of evaluators' authorizing environments. An appreciation of this complexity begins with acknowledging multiple sponsors and stakeholders operating within the authorizing environment. Also to be acknowledged is how the actions and interactions of sponsors and stakeholders have the potential—independently, collectively, and over time—to influence the evaluation scope and methodology, as well as the identification and reporting of findings and results and the use of evaluation results.

Readers of this volume will learn about the influence that authorizing environments have on state and local government evaluation; in particular, how internal and external evaluators respond to the challenges in the face of potentially conflicting and competing interests of various evaluation sponsors and stakeholders. Each of the five chapters addresses the real and potential effects that the authorizing environment can have on evaluation as a discipline and in practice.

In Chapter One, Fredericks, Carman, and Birkland discuss the historical development and evolution of evaluation practice. The authors describe the challenges to evaluation posed by political and institutional environments, particularly as they relate to implementation and management of program evaluations. The authors draw on public policy implementation models to offer readers strategies for overcoming these barriers.

Boser's story of evaluation use, in Chapter Two, is a delightful contrast with the all-too-common view that federal requirements are the primary driver of state and local evaluation efforts. Boser suggests that responding appropriately to an authorizing mandate does *not* guarantee adequate representation of program effects; she challenges the notion that local-level officials passively implement policy and report evaluation results as an exercise in placating evaluation sponsors. Using the evaluation of Even Start family literacy programs as a case example, Boser advocates involving stakeholders and integrating multiple intergovernmental perspectives in developing evaluation objectives and criteria.

In Chapter Three, Tang and colleagues provide an example of how adaptive responses to a highly complex and minimally resourced authorizing environment led to an array of systemic dividends and efficiencies. Specifically, these authors apply a combination of methods, including strategically empowering local programs over time to engage in self-assessments to fulfill state requirements for a comprehensive evaluation of the California Tobacco Control Program, or TCP. The combination not only strategically positions the state agency staff to respond fully to legislative requirements within resource constraints but is associated with better planned, more effective, and more accountable local interventions.

In Chapter Four, Guzmán and Feria examine the dynamics of a community-based organization (CBO) that becomes the medium for delivering services to individuals and for assessing and reporting on the effectiveness of those services. The authors make clear that the ecosystem within which their evaluation was conducted was crucial to the evaluation's effectiveness. They found it necessary to re-examine the hierarchical relationships within that ecosystem and renegotiate the evaluation plan to facilitate the conduct of their evaluation.

In Chapter Five, Berry, Turcotte, and Latham explore the evolution of legislative evaluation offices in the United States. As we become increasingly accustomed to living in a morass of real-time data in the information age, the need for extracting fair, thoughtful, valid, timely, and decision-oriented information from the data for sponsors and stakeholders becomes more acute than ever. These authors identify six niches that legislative program evaluation offices must fill to maintain their relevance and viability in the public policy environment.

The overarching concept of evaluation authorizing environments, as well as evaluators' ability to adapt to the needs of various sponsors and stakeholders, are developed more fully in the concluding chapter. Themes that cut across the five previous chapters are identified and interwoven to give readers a sense of both the enduring and malleable traits of the evaluation profession as it anticipates continuing its contributions to societal well-being.

Rakesh Mohan
David J. Bernstein
Maria D. Whitsett
Editors

Note

1. The views expressed in the Editors' Notes are those of the editors and do not necessarily represent those of the Washington State Joint Legislative Audit and Review Committee, Montgomery County, Maryland, or the Austin Independent School District, Texas.

References

American Evaluation Association. "Guiding Principles for Evaluators." In W. R. Shadish, D. L. Newman, M. A. Scheirer, and C. Wye (eds.), *Guiding Principles for Evaluators.* New Directions for Program Evaluation, no. 66. San Francisco: Jossey-Bass, 1995. Accessible at eval.org/Publications/publications.html.
Chelimsky, E. "The Politics of Program Evaluation." In D. S. Cordray, H. S. Bloom, and R. J. Light (eds.), *Evaluation Practice in Review.* New Directions for Program Evaluation, no. 34. San Francisco: Jossey-Bass, 1987.
Lester, J. P., and Wilds, L. J. "The Utilization of Public Policy Analysis: A Conceptual Framework." *Evaluation and Program Planning,* 1990, *13,* 313–319.
Palumbo, D. J. "Politics and Evaluation." In D. J. Palumbo (ed.), *The Politics of Program Evaluation.* Vol. 15. Thousand Oaks, Calif.: Sage, 1987.

RAKESH MOHAN *is a staff member of the Washington State Joint Legislative Audit and Review Committee. He is current chair of the State and Local Government Topical Interest Group of the AEA.*

DAVID J. BERNSTEIN *is the administrative coordinator for the Montgomery County, Maryland, Department of Finance. He is former chair of the State and Local Government Topical Interest Group of the AEA, a member of the board of directors of the American Society for Public Administration Center for Accountability and Performance, and adjunct professor of public administration at The George Washington University.*

MARIA D. WHITSETT *is the chief accountability officer for the Austin Independent School District, Texas. She is former chair of the State and Local Government Topical Interest Group and is current chair of the PreK–12 Educational Evaluation Topical Interest Group of the AEA.*

1

In today's environment, social services are provided by complex institutional and political networks comprising multiple program sponsors, implementers, and stakeholders. This environment exacerbates many problems that can occur, even in the simplest of evaluations. The authors outline the major intergovernmental and interorganizational challenges associated with doing program evaluation in today's environment and offer recommendations designed to improve evaluation efforts.

Program Evaluation in a Challenging Authorizing Environment: Intergovernmental and Interorganizational Factors

Kimberly A. Fredericks, Joanne G. Carman, Thomas A. Birkland

The program evaluation literature offers a great deal of valuable guidance on how to do program evaluation and why program evaluation is so important (Hatry, 1999; Martin and Kettner, 1996; Patton, 1997; Rossi, Freeman, and Lipsey, 1999). However, these broadly focused texts do not usually offer specific descriptions of the many challenges that are inherent in programs designed, enacted, implemented, and evaluated in multiorganizational and intergovernmental environments. This is a particularly important shortcoming, considering that programs and program evaluations must often rely on multiple sponsors, implementers, and stakeholders. Evaluators at the state and local level particularly need advice in understanding the complexity of intergovernmental and interorganizational policy evaluation. Using references to the literatures of public policy, the nonprofit sector, and interorganizational relations, this chapter outlines the major intergovernmental and interorganizational challenges associated with conducting program evaluation in today's complex authorizing environments and offers recommendations for addressing these challenges.

NEW DIRECTIONS FOR EVALUATION, no. 95, Fall 2002 © Wiley Periodicals, Inc.

Political and Institutional Environment of Program Evaluation

In recent decades, there have been at least four major changes in the political and organizational landscape of the social service delivery network in the United States: (1) an increased interest in accountability and performance measurement in all levels of government and in the nonprofit sector, (2) the delegation of social services from the federal level to states, (3) the increased reliance on nonprofit organizations for service delivery, and (4) the proliferation of complex social service provider networks made up of multiple sponsors and stakeholders.

Government Reinvention and Outcomes Measurement. A confluence of events has prompted concerns over both government and nonprofit accountability (Kearns, 1994), bringing the issues of program evaluation and performance measurement into the forefront of public management. Inflation, budget deficits, domestic spending cuts, and the conservative ideology of the 1980s brought about a renewed criticism of government bureaucracy and the efficacy of many social programs. By the late 1980s and early 1990s, the movement to "reinvent government" had gained considerable momentum by building on the experiences of the private sector with re-engineering, total quality management, and Osborn and Gaebler's landmark book *Reinventing Government* (1992), which advocated for entrepreneurial government and embraced the ideals of competitive and customer-driven government.

The reinvention movement culminated at the federal level in 1993, with the Clinton administration's National Performance Review and the Government Performance and Results Act (GPRA, 107 Stat. 285, PL 103–62, 1993). The National Performance Review—a reform initiative headed by Vice President Gore—was designed to streamline the bureaucracy, simplify rules and processes, improve coordination, and inspire innovation at the federal level (Kettl and DiIulio, 1995). GPRA was designed to refocus government attention away from agency staffing and process issues and more toward accountability, performance measurement, and results. In doing so, Section 4 of GPRA required that performance measures be specified for all federal programs in the budget for fiscal year 1999. Because many federal programs are funneled through state and local government agencies, these performance measures influence state and local government actions.

At the same time, those outside government were calling for more accountability through measuring outcomes. Many major research institutions began researching and implementing systems for implementing evaluation and enhancing accountability (Hall, Philips, Pickering, and Greenberg, 2000; Morely, Vinson, and Hatry, 2001). National nonprofit organizations began to work with their local affiliates to do outcomes measurement, and philanthropic foundations began to organize around and promote outcomes measurement (Hendricks, 2000; Patrizi and McMullan, 1999; W. K. Kellogg Foundation, n.d.).

Devolution. This renewed criticism of government and increasing focus on the outcomes of social service programs re-ignited the debate over federal and state responsibilities and devolution. The distribution of power between the federal and state governments (and in some states between the state and local governments) has been important in American politics since the founding of the republic. In the 1950s, the "public choice" school of economics argued that devolution of service delivery to the lowest level of government would allow local governments to compete on the basis of quantity of services provided and tax levels (Warner, 2001).

Devolution of power to the states gained its political momentum from the Nixon administration's New Federalism of the early 1970s, in which states were given greater discretion in policy implementation, and block grants began to replace targeted federal spending. The desire to decentralize policy and implementation stemmed from dissatisfaction with the top-down design of the Great Society programs and a perception that the federal government was too powerful and that federal programs were inflexible. This sentiment continued into the Carter administration and was reflected in general efforts to shrink the federal government and deregulate industry.

During the Reagan and Bush administration, supporters of more rapid devolution called for less government control at the federal level, while giving more flexibility, responsibility, and decision-making authority to states and localities. A new form of devolution was eventually realized during the late 1990s, as states began to operate Medicaid and Aid to Families with Dependent Children (AFDC) programs under waivers of federal laws. (Under federal waiver, states could deviate from federal standards if they could argue that a different system could improve service delivery.) Politicians sought to increase less restrictive block grants to the states, and some cuts were made in federal discretionary spending (Nathan, 1996).

This new wave of devolution culminated with the Personal Responsibility and Work Opportunity Reconciliation Act (PRWORA) of 1996, which replaced the federally funded entitlement program of AFDC with the Temporary Assistance for Needy Families (TANF) block grant to the states. PRWORA was designed to give states more latitude in defining and implementing their welfare programs. PRWORA, in many respects, has symbolized the changing relationship between the federal and state governments, as states have been able to take on more of a role in specifying the way they provide social services (Conlan, 1998; De Vita, 1999).

The proponents of devolution hoped (and its opponents feared) that the transfer of greater responsibility to states would lead to fewer constraints on program design and implementation. But regardless of the stringency or laxity of federal control, *accountability* remains important to the federal government and extends to those who expend federal funds, not just the federal agencies that dispense these funds.

Evaluators now find themselves in a rich evaluation environment (there are many devolved programs to evaluate), challenged to evaluate programs to promote effectiveness and accountability while simultaneously ensuring that accountability demands, from many different levels, do not unduly deflect the organization from its mission (Lipsky and Smith, 1989–90).

Nonprofit Organizations as Social Service Providers. Not surprisingly, these two major trends in the environment—government reinvention and devolution—prompted many to take a closer look at intergovernmental relations, including the extent to which nonprofit organizations have become the dominant providers of public social services (Lipsky and Smith, 1989–90). Although nonprofit organizations have always played a role in providing charitable services to those in need, nonprofit organizations typically relied on private funding prior to the 1960s. Changes made in 1962 and 1967 to the Social Security Act (Title XX, The Social Services Block Grant) greatly expanded the federal funding of social services and allowed state agencies to purchase services from local nonprofit and private organizations.

In addition, the Economic Opportunity Act of 1964 created a host of government programs, such as the Community Action Program, Job Corps, Neighborhood Youth Corps, and the Work Experience Program, and channeled funds to thousands of nonprofit agencies, many of which were newly created to deliver services to the poor (Coalition on Human Needs, 2001; Smith and Lipsky, 1993; Carman and Wright, 1997). As such, the character of the services being provided by nonprofit organizations changed. "Private" services, funded mostly through private philanthropic contributions, became "public" and were funded through government contracts.

Since that time, the number of nonprofit organizations serving as public service providers has, for the most part, increased, in spite of the many changes in the funding of public services and the nature of intergovernmental relations. For example, during the 1970s the Nixon administration sought to "reform and rationalize the plethora of federal assistance programs to states and localities. . . . [through] grant consolidation, general revenue sharing, and an assortment of intergovernmental management programs" (Conlan, 1998, p. 19). Many nonprofit organizations actually benefited from these policies, in that domestic spending continued to increase and many of the major entitlement programs continued to grow (De Vita, 1999). Furthermore, whereas significant cuts in the federal funding of social welfare services made by the Reagan and Bush administrations during the 1980s seriously hurt many nonprofit organizations, increases in spending for health care and housing were a boon for other nonprofit organizations (Salamon, 1999; Smith and Lipsky, 1993).

During the 1990s, federal spending for services for children and families increased under the Clinton administration, continuing federal programs' reliance on nonprofit organizations to deliver many public services. Today these include programs such as Medicare and Medicaid, the Social Services Block Grant, Community Development Block Grant, Temporary Assistance for Needy Families Block Grant, the Empowerment Zones/

Enterprise Communities Initiative, and the Home Investment Partnerships (HOME) Program for low-income housing (Clavel, Pitt, and Yin, 1997; Salamon, 1995, 1999).

Complex Networks of Service Providers. Social service providers, for the most part, must now rely on a patchwork of public and private funding sources in order to provide services. This has given rise to the development of complex institutional and political networks among social service providers, where formal and informal interorganizational relationships between funders, program implementers, regulators, evaluators, and the community are often critical to the social service provider's survival. These relationships, as well as the political and institutional environments in which they exist, can vary considerably, depending on the service field.

For example, in some service fields, such as services for children and families and services for the developmentally disabled, government agencies play an important regulatory role and are the primary funders. Many of these service providers are affiliated with state coalitions of service providers or nationally federated nonprofit organizations. Many participate in formal accreditation processes, and many seek out technical assistance from a growing web of nonprofit management resources (Gronbjerg, 1993; Smith and Lipsky, 1993; Hendricks, 2000).

In other fields, however, the political and institutional landscape within which the service provider operates may be very different. Government may play a different role, and institutional support networks may look very different as well. For example, in the field of community development, local government agencies can play a variety of roles. In some communities, they may act as partner; in other places, they may take a more adversarial position to local community development efforts. In some communities, providers of community development services are smaller and less organized, struggling with real capacity issues, and institutional support networks are more limited. In other communities, providers are larger, more organized, and enjoy considerable support from local political and institutional structures (Bratt, Keyes, Schwartz, and Vidal, 1995; Vidal, 1992).

Implications for Evaluation. We have summarized four interrelated trends in public management. The results of these trends are that social service providers are confronted with a remarkably challenging and complex environment at the same time that greater demands are being expressed for quality evaluation. This is confounded by the fact that service delivery systems have evolved in such a way that programs are designed across multiple organizations and delivered at multiple sites, such as schools, senior centers, or multiservice facilities, making service delivery and program evaluation even more complex.

These conditions serve to exacerbate many of the problems that often occur when evaluating even the simplest program. Problems include (1) stakeholders with different priorities and goals for both the program and the evaluation (Chaskin, 2000; Hall, 1999; Kubisch, Fulbright-Anderson, and Connell, 1998), (2) competing and conflicting demands for reporting and evaluation (Bernstein, 1991; Gronbjerg, 1993), (3) difficulties developing outcome measures (Campbell, 2000; Easterling, 2000), (4) data availability and data analysis issues (Coulton and Hollister, 1998), and (5) data ownership, access, sharing, and dissemination issues (Annie E. Casey Foundation, 1997).

Stakeholders comprise a diverse intra- and interorganizational network around a program. As the complexity and range of the program area grows, so too does its network of stakeholders, each of which has different agendas and priorities for both the program and the evaluation (Hall and others, 2000). These goals often conflict, providing no clear or unified message or objectives that can be used in evaluation. The process of developing outcome measures before evaluation begins can be difficult, as each stakeholder has differing needs and objectives for the evaluation that can lead to differing types of measures (Campbell, 2000; Easterling, 2000). Stakeholders often demand reporting and analysis tailored to individual stakeholder needs (Bernstein, 1991); of course, it is difficult, if not impossible, to provide customized information for each stakeholder.

With large, complex programs, multiple sites and organizations are involved in the service delivery and evaluation of the program. If data are collected at the site level, where direct service is provided, who then has ownership of those data—the site, the program, or the agency that sponsors the program? Similarly, who is allowed access to the data and results? These are difficult questions that should be answered early in the evaluation through careful planning and coordinating among stakeholders. Due to their inherent division of interests, this natural tension that occurs between various stakeholders can result in leaving one or more groups dissatisfied or disenfranchised from the evaluation unless these relationships are carefully handled through the evaluation process. This can involve an enormous amount of time, effort, and resources.

Challenges Relating to Implementation and Management of Evaluation

In addition to the intergovernmental and interorganizational challenges created by today's political and institutional environment, evaluators must confront a number of other challenges that are related to implementation and management. These include (1) variation in the capacity and commitment to evaluation, (2) the presence and interests of multiple stakeholders, (3) staff and managerial commitment, and (4) fears about cross-site comparisons and being "graded."

Different Levels of Local Capacity and Commitment. Because there are many types of service delivery organizations (state, local, special district and other governments, as well as nonprofit and for-profit organizations), there are substantial differences in organizational *capacity* to perform evaluation. Evaluation capacity is the capacity of the organization to answer the questions managers and stakeholders have about program effectiveness, efficiency, or other factors.

Capacity involves at least three aspects: (1) the availability of resources to hire and support in-house or outside evaluation staff with knowledge of appropriate evaluation strategies and methodologies; (2) agency management and staff knowledge of programmatic issues, causal theories, and the assumptions that shape service delivery; and (3) the capacity of an agency to provide evaluators with the information and the data needed to conduct the evaluation. Although most organizations possess programmatic knowledge, the resources to perform the evaluation and the systems that support the data needs for evaluation are sometimes wanting.

It is also important that programs have management information systems (MISs) that serve as information resources for *leadership* as well as management and that allow for systematic data gathering and analysis (Tuomi, 1999) rather than serve as filing systems. Often, even in the same program, MISs can vary widely from site to site in the same agency. Larger urban sites may have sophisticated relational databases and finely tuned reporting systems, whereas smaller, rural sites may keep data on spreadsheets or as paper files.

Evaluation projects can serve as the impetus for justifying, improving, and normalizing information-gathering and retrieval systems, but this is likely to happen only when an organization is able to invest in what van den Hoven (2001) calls information resource management (IRM), which goes beyond traditional systems to provide useful managerial information rather than simple data. In such cases, evaluation can serve as a prod for other managerial improvements and efficiencies (Owen and Lambert, 1998). We believe that evaluators must take care to separate their evaluator role from other potential roles in organizational development or management consulting (Smith, 1998), although some might argue that evaluation can support these broader functions.

Multiple Stakeholders. Modern conceptions of management in both the private and public sectors are that more people and groups are interested in a program than simply the program's target group (Osborne and Plastrik, 1997). These stakeholders often represent diffuse interests that are spatially and organizationally dispersed. Together, all players who have a claim to a program form the interorganizational and intraorganizational linkages that make up the program's network. Organizations outside the direct area of a program exhibit interorganizational linkages. These organizations include funding sources, suppliers, accrediting organizations, regulatory and oversight agencies, and referral sources (Hall, 1999). Conversely, stakeholders directly involved in the program have intraorganizational linkages that include but are not limited to clients, service providers, and parent, affiliate, or satellite organizations, as would be the case in large social service programs. The complexity of the network and the program increases as programs becomes larger, creating a complex web of relationships within the network. Although it has not been widely studied in the public sector, research in the private arena has shown that these linkages increase the overall support and the perceived legitimacy of the program, which ultimately results in increased survivability of the program (Baum and Oliver, 1991; Uzzi, 1997). Understanding and working through these networks can become a major challenge to program evaluation.

Staff and Managerial Commitment. Managerial and staff commitment or buy-in to the evaluation is important. Managers are positioned to shape the overall evaluation environment. Management styles can range from a style that is adversarial and intimidating, to one that focuses on oversight, monitoring, and accountability, to one that promotes organizational learning and programmatic improvement. Managers are also in a position to send messages to program staff regarding the importance and utility of the evaluation. The extent to which management can help facilitate staff commitment to the evaluation is extremely important; staff often possess critical knowledge about program operations and staff are often called upon to collect data for the evaluation (Bell, 1994; Goggin and others, 1990; Gray and Associates, 1998).

Fears About Cross-Site Comparisons and Being Graded. Some organizations resist evaluation, and they take steps ranging from foot-dragging to outright refusal to cooperate with evaluators as they evaluate programmatic outcomes. Many program stakeholders, particularly front-line staff or direct service providers, may view evaluation as grading or even as punishment (Posavac, 1994; Easterling, 2000); they will cooperate reluctantly, if at all, with evaluation efforts. This foot-dragging may result from staff dissatisfaction with management, a belief by management and staff that evaluation is a waste of time, or, in particular, fears that the evaluation will damage the organization's political standing with its clients, stakeholders, or funders. But one must also admit to the possibility that what appears to be foot-dragging may in fact be "strategic delay" (Goggin and others, 1990) that seeks to improve evaluation outcomes by signaling to evaluation designers that the assumptions of the project may require modification. Creating an "evaluation culture," as described later, can help promote this sort of useful feedback while avoiding efforts to delay or stymie evaluation.

Implications for Evaluation. The implementation and management challenges we review in this chapter underscore the importance of performing an evaluability assessment before proceeding with a full-fledged evaluation project (Wholey, 1979). At a minimum, evaluators are counseled to avoid taking on projects where sufficient resources are lacking (Rog, 1997). Even when sufficient resources are dedicated to evaluation, those who are involved in the evaluation project need to make a formal and explicit commitment to the evaluation up front. Evaluators need to be prepared for unpredictable stakeholder reactions to the evaluation project and for stakeholder reactions to any managerial actions taken as a result of the evaluation project. Such challenges are multiplied if the broadest range of stakeholders is not identified and at least informed of the evaluation program (Weiss, 1998). Stakeholder analysis is complicated by the complexity of the program and service delivery networks, and the resulting formal and informal systems created to structure and nurture these relationships (Krackhardt, 1990).

We believe that involving stakeholders at the early stages of evaluation planning can reassure them that they are not being graded per se but that the primary focus is on improving program performance. Such improvements would redound to the benefit of all stakeholders (Turpin and Sinacore, 1991). Efforts to build trust and open communication are key to this endeavor because without trust, cooperative relationships cannot be established and maintained (Child and Faulkner, 1998). Without these relationships, the evaluator is not able to fully gain access to the program network and therefore will not have a thorough understanding of the program or the ability to complete a through and meaningful evaluation.

Evaluation efforts often falter, and the reliability of the evaluation results can be questioned if management and staff are not committed to the evaluation process. Evaluations that are initiated by higher management, in collaboration with key stakeholders, tend to be much more successful than those initiated solely by a funder or government agency. As Russ-eft (1999) and Chelimsky (1987) note, evaluation is deeply imbued with politics, and the evaluator must be fully aware of the political aspects of the evaluation process and its outcomes. Understanding the political context of evaluation is necessary if one is to understand why there are fears about comparisons between program sites.

As noted here, it is important to involve or at a very minimum inform stakeholders during all aspects of planning and executing the evaluation, in order to facilitate the cooperation of stakeholders and to assuage any fears. If resistance is expressed during the planning stage, it is possible to diagnose and correct perceived problems before the research design is set and data gathering begins. For example, local sites often want to know how individual-level data will be stored and analyzed anonymously, whether data will be aggregated or disaggregated in reports, what data will be reported, and what the "real" goal of the evaluation is, beyond the usual assertion that the intent of evaluation is programmatic improvement to the benefit of stakeholders. Other problems may be revealed during evaluation planning, such as resource constraints (money, equipment, or personnel) or managerial problems. These problems can influence the success of an evaluation project and must be addressed carefully. However, the evaluator should do so within the broader mission of the evaluation project, which is learning about the *outcomes* of programs. Although managerial and resource problems will be an issue, the evaluator is not charged with fixing resource and management problems. However, the evaluation may result in the organization initiating changes on its own.

Overcoming Challenges: An Implementation Design Approach

Although there are considerable impediments to successful evaluation in an intergovernmental and interorganizational setting, several ways to think about designing complex evaluations that take advantage of the literature on public policy implementation and recognize the importance of the larger political environment within which social service providers operate (Pressman and Wildavsky, 1973; Van Horn and Van Meter, 1976; Bowen, 1982; Mazmanian and Sabatier, 1983; Sabatier, 1986; Goggin and others, 1990; Ingram and Schneider, 1990).

Local Capacity, Staff, and Managerial Commitment. Malcolm Goggin and his colleagues (Goggin and others, 1990) advanced a communications model of policy implementation. We borrow concepts from this model to show the key relationships between the evaluating agency, the non-profit service delivery agency, and what Goggin and others call the "affected groups" or stakeholders. Figure 1.1 illustrates the key linkages in a communications model of evaluation.

Goggin and his colleagues argue that clear messages sent by credible officials and received by receptive implementers who have/are given sufficient resources and who implement policies supported by affected groups lead to implementation success (1990). Clear messages would explain what evaluation is, why it is being done, and how the evaluation will improve local management and delivery of services and lead to better outcomes. Credibility derives from either the legal authority of the agency to compel compliance with its directives or from the overall record of the agency in initiating and completing useful evaluation projects. Optimally, credibility is a combination of these two elements.

In Figure 1.1, we show the importance of messages to and from stakeholders. Such groups are important to evaluation success and must be provided with information about the nature and benefits of program evaluation so that they can support the broad aims of evaluation efforts. In particular, the stakeholders should be committed to the evaluation project while also having the capacity (or being assisted in building the capacity) to provide important data and background implementation to the evaluators. This connection may be closest between the delivery agency and the stakeholders, as this is often a provider-client relationship with a fairly well-known group of clients.

However, no amount of clarity or commitment can make up for inadequate resources. The capacity of small agencies and nonprofits to fully participate in evaluation projects is often limited by constrained resources. Money is most often associated with resources, but time and staff expertise are also important resources that, if not available locally, must be provided by the sponsoring agency in order to promote successful evaluation. Of course, in any evaluation project the delivery agency will need to devote

Figure 1.1. A Communications Model of Relationships in Program Evaluation

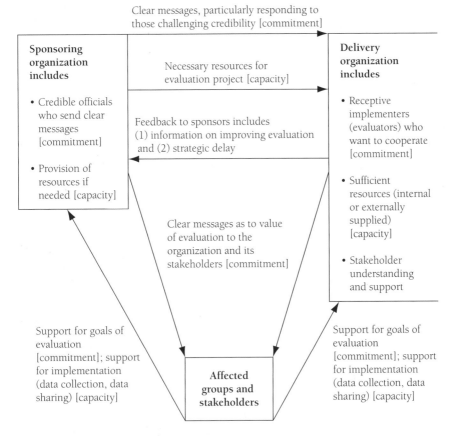

Source: Concepts adopted and modified from Goggin, Bowman, Lester, and O'Toole, 1990.

some of its resources to the effort—resources such as staff time to gather files or fill out surveys. Again, this calls for balancing the resource burdens.

Such communication is enhanced by including representatives from multiple sites and organizations on the evaluation team and by providing regular, routine communications with all participants in evaluation. By doing so, the credibility of all messages about the evaluation process will be enhanced.

Multiple Stakeholders. In an effort to understand the complex relationships involved in multiorganizational evaluation, evaluators would be well served by conducting a network analysis (Powell, 1990; Krackhardt, 1990; Uzzi, 1997). This analysis would elicit the formal and informal structures in the program and the nature and density of the linkages between stakeholders. By examining the influential stakeholders within a program and their ties with other organizations within and outside the purview of the program, an evaluator can better understand the behavior of the organization and hence the program (Powell, 1990). The important functions of a program take place within a web of network linkages that are both formal (consistent with the organizational chart) and informal (ad hoc) relationships. Analysis of this type allows one to better understand the resources available to a stakeholder within a program, which often provides insight into the power and influence that a stakeholder has both in the organization and in the evaluation (Powell, 1990). With a better understanding of the network map of a program, this type of analysis would aid in increasing trust, commitment, information access, validity, and the ultimate utilization of evaluation results.

Managerial Commitment. Evaluators may also take steps to ensure that multiple levels of an organization—top managers, middle management, and staff—are committed to the project. Similar efforts may be pursued across agencies to promote commitment across organizations. This is building an evaluation culture in which all members of an organization are committed to the purposes and goals of evaluation projects. Again, although this is a generic feature of management and of any program evaluation project, this culture-building becomes more challenging when one is working in a complex program with a vast network of stakeholders. Managerial and staff commitment can create this culture through routine reminders that the evaluation is important and through the dissemination of ongoing reports and information about the evaluation.

As we have noted, it is important in the implementation process to send a credible message to those charged with implementation (Goggin and others, 1990) and, in particular, to indicate strong managerial support for the evaluation project. A lack of support for evaluation at the organizational or agency level, whether due to outright opposition to the project or more subtle indifference, can be fatal to the evaluation effort. Those who work in an evaluation unit or as an evaluation consultant must carefully consider whether top-level management support in each area can be sustained throughout the project. Such commitment is often difficult to sustain in the public sector, where top managers are political appointees who serve for relatively short periods and where new managers sometimes quash programs begun under previous management simply because they have no ownership in the old project. In organizations with a history of rapid managerial change and what permanent staff may perceive as a managerial disposition toward management fads (Wilkinson and Redman, 1994; Zorn, Page, and Cheney, 2000), the credibility of management's ongoing commitment to an evaluation project must be continually maintained.

To combat potential loss of managerial commitment, it is important for the evaluator to ensure that managerial dedication is ongoing and consistent by keeping key managers involved in the project planning and execution (Weiss, 1998). It is also useful to appoint a steering committee with representation from all stakeholders involved in the program and those entities that would be involved in the project. A steering committee is similar to Patton's concept of a task force involving multiple stakeholders that provides input throughout an evaluation (Patton, 1987). This creates continued support from all those involved and creates program contacts to assist with possible data gathering or other project initiatives; it also provides for a liaison between the evaluator and program sites. This contact may begin to generate broad-based ownership of the project and promote its usefulness throughout the organization. In addition, a feedback mechanism can be created between staff and the evaluation team, which can improve implementation (Patrizi and McMullan, 1999). Finally, it is important to clarify who will implement the evaluation and why it is being done before beginning the project. This is accomplished through constant communication to all immediate stakeholders of project details and plans.

Fears About Comparisons Across Sites. Effective communication between the designers of an evaluation project and managers at program sites is central to successful evaluation. Communication with the sites can be significantly improved in several ways.

First, it is important to explain to all those involved what evaluation is, why it is being done, and how the evaluation will improve local management and delivery of services and lead to better outcomes. Second, it is crucial to stress to pertinent stakeholders what evaluation is *not*. Many of the individuals involved at all levels of the program will view evaluation with suspicion. Stakeholders will need to be educated about the difference between measuring outputs, which may be relatively easy to measure, and outcomes, which may be harder to measure. After all, it is relatively simple to measure how many hours are devoted to, say, an adult literacy program, but more difficult to measure the outcomes of such effort. Third, it is important to include all stakeholders from various programs on the project planning team and the evaluation team, as this will foster trust and commitment from all levels. Fourth, it is crucial to establish routine lines of communication with the central and local evaluation teams. To the greatest extent possible, communications should be relatively informal. Program staff should be able to phone or e-mail members of the evaluation team as needed and should feel comfortable about doing so without having to "go through channels" or any other bureaucratic process. Finally, it is essential to provide regular updates to all stakeholders, whether directly or indirectly involved in the evaluation project, to again maintain trust, commitment, and communication. This can be accomplished through a paper newsletter, a weekly e-mail report, or a dedicated Web page.

Conclusion

Program evaluation is an important function of government and of organizations entrusted with using public resources to achieve policy goals. Evaluation is a very challenging task, as the literature suggests. The challenge is further compounded when evaluators must account for multiple sets of organizations, clients, stakeholders, and funders, often with differing and incompatible goals. Intergovernmental evaluation is challenging because programs are complex and multifaceted. Large evaluations have mostly occurred in large public programs such as welfare or educational reform that involve a diverse and complex interorganizational network. To understand such public programs, evaluators must understand and account for the full range of stakeholders in the program and in the evaluation process. Through an interorganizational evaluation framework, relevant stakeholders can be identified, the nature and diversity of the program can be elicited, and problems and concerns can be addressed to make the evaluation useful and successful.

Evaluation challenges, once identified, can be effectively overcome. Quality evaluation can proceed in the face of these challenges, and, indeed, interorganizational evaluation can contribute to program design, program implementation, and the overall management of the agencies charged with program delivery.

References

Annie E. Casey Foundation. *Evaluating Comprehensive Community Change: A Report of the Annie E. Casey Foundation's March 1997 Research and Evaluation Conference.* Baltimore: Annie E. Casey Foundation, 1997.

Baum, J.A.C., and Oliver, C. "Institutional Linkages and Organizational Mortality." *Administrative Science Quarterly,* 1991, *36,* 187–218.

Bell, J. B. "Managing Evaluation Projects Step by Step." In J. S. Wholey, H. P. Hatry, and K. E. Newcomer (eds.), *Handbook of Practical Program Evaluation.* San Francisco: Jossey-Bass, 1994.

Bernstein, S. R. "Contracted Services: Issues for the Nonprofit Agency Manager." *Nonprofit and Voluntary Sector Quarterly,* 1991, *20,* 429–443.

Bowen, E. R. "The Pressman-Wildavsky Paradox: Four Addenda or Why Models Based on Probability Theory Can Predict Implementation Success and Suggest Useful Tactical Advice for Implementors." *Journal of Public Policy,* 1982, *2*(1), 1–22.

Bratt, R. G., Keyes, L. C., Schwartz, A., and Vidal, A. C. *Confronting the Management Challenge: Affordable Housing in the Nonprofit Sector.* New York: New School for Social Research, Community Development Research Center, 1995.

Campbell, D. "Outcomes Assessment and the Paradox of Accountability." Presented at the meeting of the Association for Research on Nonprofit Organizations and Voluntary Action, New Orleans, Nov. 16–18, 2000.

Carman, J. G., and Wright, D. J. *Prologue to the Empowerment Zone/Enterprise Community Initiative.* Albany, N.Y.: Nelson A. Rockefeller Institute of Government, State University of New York, 1997.

Chaskin, R. J. "Two-Tiered Evaluation in the Neighborhood and Family Initiative: Dilemmas of Implementation." Presented at the annual meeting of the Association for Public Policy Analysis and Management, University of Chicago, Chapin Hall Center for Children, 2000.

Chelimsky, E. "What Have We Learned about the Politics of Program Evaluation?" *Evaluation Practice,* 1987, *8,* 5–21.

Child, J., and Faulkner, D. *Strategies of Co-operation: Managing Alliances, Networks, and Joint Ventures.* New York: Oxford University Press, 1998.

Clavel, P., Pitt, J., and Yin, J. "The Community Option in Urban Policy." *Urban Affairs Review,* 1997, *32*(4), 435–438.

Coalition on Human Needs. "History of the Social Services Block Grant." 2001. Accessible at chn.org/titlexx/historytitlexx.html.

Conlan, T. J. *New Federalism: Intergovernmental Reform and Political Change from Nixon to Reagan*. Washington, D.C.: Brookings Institution, 1998.

Coulton, C., and Hollister, R. "Measuring Comprehensive Community Initiative Outcomes Using Data Available for Small Areas." In K. Fulbright-Anderson, A. C. Kubisch, and J. P. Connell (eds.), *New Approaches to Evaluating Community Initiatives*, Vol. 2: *Theory, Measurement and Analysis*. Queenstown, Md.: Aspen Institute, 1998.

De Vita, C. J. "Nonprofits and Devolution: What Do We Know?" In E. T. Boris and C. E. Steurele (eds.), *Nonprofits and Government: Collaboration and conflict*. Washington, D.C.: The Urban Institute, 1999.

Easterling, D. "Using Outcome Evaluation to Guide Grant Making: Theory, Reality, And Possibilities." *Nonprofit and Voluntary Sector Quarterly*, 2000, 29(3), 482–486.

Goggin, M. L., Bowman, A. O'M., Lester, J. P., and O'Toole, L. J., Jr. *Implementation Theory and Practice: Toward a Third Generation*. Glenview, Ill.: Scott, Foresman, 1990.

Gray, S. T., and Associates (eds.). *Evaluation with Power: Developing Organizational Effectiveness, Empowerment and Excellence*. San Francisco: Jossey-Bass, 1998.

Gronbjerg, K. A. *Understanding Nonprofit Funding*. San Francisco: Jossey-Bass, 1993.

Hall, M. H., Philips, S. D., Pickering, D. I., and Greenberg, L. "The Capacity for Accountability: An Exploratory Study of the Needs of Nonprofit Organizations for Evaluation Resources." Presented at the annual conference of the Association for Research on Nonprofit and Voluntary Action, New Orleans, Nov. 16–18, 2000.

Hall, R. H. *Organizations: Structures, Processes, and Outcomes*. Englewood Cliffs, N.J.: Prentice Hall, 1999.

Hatry, H. P. *Performance Measurement: Getting Results*. Washington, D.C.: Urban Institute Press, 1999.

Hendricks, M. "Outcomes Measurement in the Nonprofit Sector: Recent Developments, Incentives, and Challenges." Presented at the American Society for Public Administration, Center for Accountability and Performance, Symposium on Leadership of Results-Oriented Management in Government, George Washington University, Feb. 11–12, 2000.

Ingram, H., and Schneider, A. "Improving Implementation through Framing Smarter Statutes." *Journal of Public Policy* 1990, 10(1), 67–87.

Kearns, K. P. "The Strategic Management of Accountability in Nonprofit Organizations: An Analytical Framework." *Public Administration Review*, 1994, 54(2), 185–192.

Kettl, D. F., and DiIulio, J. J. (eds.). *Inside the Reinvention Machine*. Washington, D.C.: Brookings Institution, 1995.

Krackhardt, D. "Assessing the Political Landscape: Structure, Cognition, and Power in Organizations." *Administrative Science Quarterly*, 1990, 35, 342–369.

Kubisch, A. C., Fulbright-Anderson, K., and Connell, J. P. "Evaluating Community Initiative: A Progress Report." In K. Fulbright-Anderson, A. C. Kubisch, and J. P. Connell (eds.), *New Approaches To Evaluating Community Initiatives*, Vol. 2: *Theory, Measurement and Analysis*. Queenstown, Md.: Aspen Institute, 1998.

Lipsky, M., and Smith, S. R. "Nonprofit Organizations, Government, and the Welfare State." *Political Science Quarterly*, 1989–90, 104(4), 625–648.

Martin, L. J., and Kettner, P. M. *Measuring the Performance of Human Service Programs*. Sage Human Service Guides no. 71. Thousand Oaks, Calif.: Sage, 1996.

Mazmanian, D., and Sabatier, P. *Implementation and Public Policy*. Glenview, Ill.: Scott, Foresman, 1983.

Morley, E., Vinson, E., and Hatry, H. P. *Outcome Measurement in Nonprofit Organizations: Current Practices and Recommendations*. Waldorf, Md.: INDEPENDENT SECTOR, 2001.

Nathan, R. P. "The 'Nonprofitization' Movement as a Form of Devolution." In D. F. Burlingame, W. A. Diaz, W. F. Ilchman, and Associates (eds.), *Capacity for Change? The Nonprofit World in the Age of Devolution*. Indianapolis: Indiana University, Center on Philanthropy, 1996.

Osborne, D. E., and Gaebler, T. A. *Reinventing Government: How the Entrepreneurial Spirit Is Transforming the Public Sector.* New York: Penguin Books, 1992.

Osborne, D. E., and Plastrik, P. *Banishing Bureaucracy: The Five Strategies for Reinventing Government.* New York: Penguin Books, 1997.

Owen, J. M., and Lambert, F. C. "Evaluation and the Information Needs of Organizational Leaders." *American Journal of Evaluation,* 1998, *19*(3), 355–365.

Patrizi, P., and McMullan, B. J. "Realizing the Potential of Program Evaluation." *Foundation News and Commentary,* 1999, *40*(2), 30–35. Accessible at cof.org/foundationnews/0599/potential.htm.

Patton, M. Q. "Evaluation's Political Inherence: Practical Implications for Design and Use." In D. J. Palumbo (ed.), *The Politics of Program Evaluation,* Vol. 15, 100–105. Thousand Oaks, Calif.: Sage, 1987.

Patton, M. Q. *Utilization-Focused Evaluation: The New Century Text.* Thousand Oaks, Calif.: Sage, 1997.

Posavac, E. J. "Misusing Program Evaluation by Asking the Wrong Question." In C. J. Stevens and M. Dial (eds.), *Preventing the Misuse of Evaluation.* New Directions for Program Evaluation, no. 64. San Francisco: Jossey-Bass, 1994.

Powell, W. W. "Neither Market nor Hierarchy: Network Forms of Organization." *Research in Organizational Behavior,* 1990, *12,* 295–336.

Pressman, J., and Wildavsky, A. *Implementation.* Berkeley: University of California Press, 1973.

Rog, D. J. "When NOT to Do an Outcome Evaluation: Assessing the Evaluability of a Program." In R. E. Stake (Chair), "Grounds for Turning Down a Handsome Evaluation Contract." Symposium conducted at the meeting of the American Educational Research Association, Chicago, 1997. Cited in N. L. Smith, "Professional Reasons for Declining an Evaluation Contract." *American Journal of Evaluation,* 1998, *19*(2), 177–190.

Rossi, P. H., Freeman, H. E., and Lipsey, M. W. *Evaluation: A Systematic Approach.* Thousand Oaks, Calif.: Sage, 1999.

Russ-eft, D. "Commentary: Can this Evaluation Be Saved?" *American Journal of Evaluation,* 1999, *20*(3), 590–597.

Sabatier, P. A. "Top-Down and Bottom-Up Approaches in Implementation Research: A Critical Analysis and Suggested Synthesis." *Journal of Public Policy,* 1986, *6*(1), 21–48.

Salamon, L. A. *Partners in Public Service: Government-Nonprofit Relations in the Modern Welfare State.* Baltimore: Johns Hopkins University Press, 1995.

Salamon, L. A. *America's Nonprofit Sector: A Primer.* New York: The Foundation Center, 1999.

Smith, N. L. "Professional Reasons for Declining an Evaluation Contract." *American Journal of Evaluation,* 1998, *19*(2), 177–190.

Smith, S. R., and Lipsky, M. *Nonprofits for Hire: The Welfare State in the Age of Contracting.* Cambridge, Mass.: Harvard University Press, 1993.

Tuomi, I. "Data Is More than Knowledge: Implications of the Reversed Knowledge Hierarchy for Knowledge Management and Organizational Memory." *Journal of Management Information Systems,* 1999, *16*(3), 103–117.

Turpin, R. S., and Sinacore, J. M. (eds.). *Multisite Evaluations.* San Francisco: Jossey-Bass, 1991.

Uzzi, B. "Social Structure and Competition in Interfirm Networks: The Paradox of Embeddedness." *Administrative Science Quarterly,* 1997, *42,* 35–67.

van den Hoven, J. "Information Resource Management: Foundation for Knowledge Management." *Information Systems Management,* 2001, *18*(2), 80–83.

Van Horn, C. E., and Van Meter, D. S. "The Implementation of Intergovernmental Policy." In C. O. Jones and R. D. Thomas (eds.), *Public Policy Making in a Federal System.* Thousand Oaks, Calif.: Sage, 1976.

Vidal, A. C. *Rebuilding Communities: A National Study of Community Development Corporations.* New York: Community Development Research Center, New School for Social Research, 1992.

Warner, M. "State Policy under Devolution: Redistribution and Centralization." *National Tax Journal,* 2001, *54*(3), 541–547.

Weiss, C. H. *Evaluation.* Englewood Cliffs, N.J.: Prentice Hall, 1998.

Wholey, J. S. *Evaluation: Promise and Performance.* Washington D.C.: Urban Institute, 1979.

Wilkinson, A., and Redman, T. "The Problems with Quality Management: The View of Managers." *Total Quality Management,* 1994, *5*(6), 397–406.

W. K. Kellogg Foundation. *Evaluation Handbook.* Collateral Management Company, Battle Creek, Mich., no. 1203 (n.d.).

Zorn, T. E., Page, D. J., and Cheney, G. "Nuts about Change." *Management Communication Quarterly,* 2000, *13*(4), 515–566.

KIMBERLY A. FREDERICKS *and* JOANNE G. CARMAN *are doctoral candidates in the Department of Public Administration and Policy, Nelson A. Rockefeller College of Public Affairs and Policy, University at Albany, State University of New York.*

THOMAS A. BIRKLAND *is associate professor of political science and public administration and policy, as well as director of the Center for Policy Research in the Nelson A. Rockefeller College of Public Affairs and Policy, University at Albany, State University of New York.*

2

Although the authorizing environment may dictate the nature and use of evaluations, state and locally conducted evaluation provides a distinct lens for understanding the conditions affecting program implementation and the outcomes of programs under study. The learning that transpires at the state and local government levels through evaluation can motivate stakeholders to use evaluation to influence the policy agenda.

Evaluation Across an Intergovernmental Context: Issues Raised Through Different Perspectives on Even Start

Susan Boser

For state and local government, the federal authorizing environment significantly affects the evaluation design of programs by mandating such elements as what evaluation shall be conducted, by and for whom, and with what resources. However, although the authorizing environment may dictate the nature and use of evaluations, state and local governments' response should not be construed as passive implementation of federal directives. Indeed, state and locally conducted evaluation provides a distinct lens for understanding the conditions affecting program implementation and the outcomes of those programs. In particular, the state and local perspectives may be more adept at identifying the subtleties of context that influence program operations and identifying short-term outcomes that serve as benchmarks toward longer-term goals. And just as evaluation and research can be used to justify a particular agenda at the national level, the learning that transpires at the state and local government levels through evaluation can motivate actors at those levels to use evaluation to influence the policy agenda.

Analysis of national, state, and local evaluations of the Even Start family literacy programs illustrates this point. The Even Start projects have been intensively evaluated since originally authorized by federal legislation in 1988 (Morrow, Tracey, and Maxwell, 1995). The initial legislation mandated evaluation of these programs at different intergovernmental levels. It established and funded broad-based national evaluation of program outcomes to inform future policy. In addition, Congress required that local evaluation for local audiences be conducted in order to support program improvement; the local educational agencies seeking to operate an Even Start program are mandated to set aside a specific portion of the program budget to fund this evaluation (U.S. Department of Education, 1998).

This chapter presents the scope of the national evaluation efforts of Even Start to date, summarizing the evaluation strategies, rationale, intended audience, and findings. In addition, it describes the mandate for Even Start evaluation at the state and local levels. I argue that evaluation conducted at the state and local levels offered different lenses for understanding the context of the program implementation, as well as different understandings of the relevant domains for evaluation. Against this background, I describe the intention, design, and lessons learned from the New York State Longitudinal Case Study and discuss the implications this example has for evaluation practice in the intergovernmental context.

Evaluation Structured by the Authorizing Context: The Case of Even Start

Even Start programs have been among the well-funded and highly evaluated of the literacy programs established by federal legislation. These programs also demonstrate many of the characteristics reflective of the family support movement for human service provision, in that services are community-based, family-focused and -driven, flexible, strength-based, and individualized (Bruner, 1994). Even Start thus illustrates characteristics associated with being strongly constituted by both the federal authorizing environment and the local implementing environment, with the state mediating between the two. As such, it provides a useful case for exploring evaluation practice in the intergovernmental milieu.

Overview of Even Start Programs. Even Start is among the premiere models for the delivery of family literacy services in the United States. Established by federal legislation in 1988 as a demonstration project, Even Start was reauthorized in 1994 by the Improving America's Schools Act (PL 103–382). As of 1998, over 637 programs were in place nationwide, serving approximately 33,000 families (U.S. Department of Education, 1998).

The goal of Even Start is to help break cycles of poverty and illiteracy through early childhood education, adult education, and parenting education to families. Several particular features mark Even Start. A two-generation program, Even Start serves both parents and their children from birth through age eight. It also targets those most in need economically and educationally within a geographic service area, offering support services to address barriers to education. These services may include advocacy and linkage to other family support mechanisms, problem solving and crisis resolution, and transportation (St. Pierre, Layzer, and Barnes, 1995). Per PL

100–297 and as amended by PL 105–277 and PL 106–554, all Even Start programs provide the following four components (New York State Even Start Family Literacy Partnership, 2001):

1. Interactive literacy activities between parents and their children
2. Training for parents regarding how to be the primary teachers for their children and full partners in the education of their children
3. Adult literacy training that leads to economic self-sufficiency
4. Age-appropriate education for children

Programs vary considerably across sites (U.S. Department of Education, 1998), with some of this variation being a function of the funding design itself. Even Start programs are eligible for federal funding for eight years, with grants awarded in two four-year funding cycles. The legislation requires a local match in resources, which must increase proportionately over the duration of the federal grant. This match is often provided in the form of concrete, direct service and often constitutes specific program components. This policy reflects an underlying assumption that the program should be community-focused, using other established community services, with other local resources eventually coming to fully support the program.

National Evaluation of Even Start. Within the field of family literacy, the Even Start projects have been the most intensively evaluated of all programs. The appropriations for Even Start totaled $124 million by 1998, with almost $4 million established for a national evaluation of the program (U.S. Department of Education, 1998).

Since Even Start first began in 1989, it has been the subject of three national evaluation studies. The first took place between 1990 and 1995 and the second between 1994 and 1998; the third began in 1997 and is slated for completion in 2002. Research questions for each evaluation have focused on defining the populations served, determining the range and nature of program implementation, and evaluating participant outcomes. Each of these national evaluations has built on the previous effort, extending a similar evaluation design. This design entails two main thrusts: collection and analysis of common data from all Even Start programs and participants and an in-depth study of a select number of Even Start projects (St. Pierre, Layzer, and Barnes, 1995; St. Pierre, Ricciuti, and Tao, 1997).

The data collected from all Even Start programs include information about program implementation, activities and costs, and demographic data on the program participants. The first and second national evaluations focused on program and participant descriptors; the third broadened its focus to include results from standardized tests and family progress indicators such as economic self-sufficiency, family functioning, and parent-child relationships (St. Pierre, Ricciuti, and Tao, 1997).

Although varying in some of the details, each national evaluation has used an in-depth study of a select number of programs to capture a more detailed perspective of outcomes for children and parents as a result of program participation. Each study used an experimental design with randomly assigned control groups and pre- and posttesting on key measures. Criteria for success included gains in adult literacy, achievement of general education development (GED) certificates, gains in school readiness for young children, and improvement in parenting skills. Criteria were measured using standardized reading and literacy tests for adults and standardized assessments of school readiness for children (St. Pierre, Ricciuti, and Tao, 1997).

The results of the third national evaluation were not yet available at the time of this writing. However, the second one demonstrated that overall, the Even Start programs met the specified criteria for adult literacy, school readiness for children, and parenting improvement only to a limited degree (St. Pierre, Layzer, and Barnes, 1995; St. Pierre, Swartz, Murray, and Deck, 1996; Tao, Schwartz, St. Pierre, and Tarr, 1997; U.S. Department of Education, 1998). The findings are summarized as follows:

- Adult Even Start participants achieved significant gains on standardized literacy measures; however, the participants in the control groups from the in-depth study did, too.
- Adult program participants achieved significant gains in obtaining GED certificates when compared to the control groups.
- Children in Even Start made significant gains on measures of language development and reading readiness, compared to children in the control groups. However, when followed through preschool or kindergarten, the control group children's performance on these measures caught up with those shown by program participants.
- Parents in Even Start made significant gains on measures of parenting skills, home environment, and expectations for their children. The control groups demonstrated inconsistent results.

Thus the evaluation could not conclusively state that progress on the key program success indicators, other than attainment of GED certificates, could be attributed to participation in the Even Start programs (U.S. Department of Education, 1998).

Local Evaluation of Even Start. In addition to mandating the national studies, the federal legislation authorizing Even Start requires each project to conduct a local evaluation (PL 103–382, Sec. 1205). The goal of this local evaluation is to provide information to the local stakeholders for program improvement (U.S. Department of Education, 1998). State evaluation is not required by the legislation. The state role in the local evaluation process varies widely, with some states determining the type, extent, and methods of the local evaluation and other state agencies choosing to allow this to be locally determined (U.S. Department of Education, 1998).

New York allows for local determination of evaluation design and focus, though it provides resources and technical assistance to programs and evaluators to enhance the quality of local evaluation. As a local evaluator for Even Start programs in New York in the late 1990s, I had the opportunity to participate in regional, state, and national meetings for Even Start evaluators. I also talked with other local Even Start evaluators and program coordinators and exchanged evaluation reports with them. Drawing on this experience, as well as a review of the literature, I share my observations on the local perspective of how the authorizing context intersects with evaluation in the section that follows.

Local Perspectives on the National Evaluation

Essentially, local experience with the Even Start program, as well as some of the local evaluations themselves, provided local and state coordinators with a different lens for understanding how Even Start affected participants' lives than that depicted by the national evaluation. Many state and local stakeholders maintain that the absence of evidence of stronger impact was, in fact, the result of the methodological design of the national evaluation itself and the evaluation's inability to represent the reality of a complex social program.

The local perspective argues that both the aggregation of data across widely varying sites and the experimental design for the in-depth study fail to capture evidence of stronger impact because of the absence of contextual elements. Indeed, the diversity across these programs is such that it renders meaningless the results of a broad-brush evaluation approach.

Three lines of reasoning support this position. First, the diversity among program participants presents challenges to developing evaluation constructs that adequately capture the program's impact. Second, this challenge is compounded by the perspective of local staff involved in data gathering for the national evaluation and the ways in which they interpret their tasks. Third, the evaluation is further challenged by the diversity across programs as they adapt to local resources and needs in implementation. Some of these arguments have been articulated in the literature; I include these next, as well as my observations as an evaluator with local Even Start programs.

Measurement Constructs and Processes for a Diverse Population. The literacy field continues to debate the definition of literacy and how to conceptualize authentic progress toward literacy. Some argue for a definition reflecting the cultural variation among individuals, groups, and even societies. The same parties also assert that evaluation of literacy programs must therefore take into account the literacy context of the individual (Ryan, Geissler, and Knell, 1994).

Many local programs would agree that literacy must be understood in the context of the individual participant if that program is to successfully engage the participant. Programs must respond to and work with individuals as they define literacy and their literacy goals. Program participants' literacy goals are a function of their values, their contexts, and their lives, which necessarily vary widely across people and programs. For example, for some, literacy might entail obtaining a GED certificate to qualify for further vocational training. Others may find such a goal beyond their reach; for them, literacy might mean being able to help their children with homework or to read circulars that identify items on sale at the local market. Still others, such as high-functioning individuals who are literate in a different culture but struggling with poverty in the United States, may be seeking English as a second language. Programs must respond to the relevance that literacy has for the individual participants, as it has a direct impact on motivation for participation. Individuals who do not see the program supporting the goals they have for themselves generally will not participate.

Similarly, evaluation activities must take into account this diversity to represent accurately the impact of the program. Measurement constructs that define literacy progress as "achievement on standardized measures" or as "attainment of a GED certificate" may miss other indicators of literacy progress. In using standardized measures, the national evaluation must assume narrow constructs of what constitutes literacy and cannot be sensitive enough to measure the rich diversity of what actually constitutes literacy for a population this diverse.

Characteristics of program participants vary widely both within and across sites in many other ways as well. These include variation in range of skills, proficiency in English, social and economic goals, and the presence of special needs, among others (Brooks and Hayes, 1998; U.S. Department of Education, 1998). Given that Even Start is charged with serving those most in need educationally and economically, standardized measures and processes may not be sensitive enough to capture substantial gains in other ways as well.

For example, program participants may include a socially isolated adult with significant developmental disabilities and psychological problems. Often such individuals demonstrate significant suspicion of educators and resistance to activities such as taking pretests. For a participant like this, a substantial engagement process, sometimes over a period of months, must take place so a pretest can be administered. Similarly, willingness to come to the center and take the pretest in itself reflects a successful engagement process, which is one of the short-term objectives for the program; it also reflects a benchmark of progress for that participant. Given its mandate to serve those most in need, local Even Start programs will consider the percentage of such individuals who are successfully engaged in center-based activities to be one indicator of its success. Other local stakeholders, such as school systems and social service agencies, also see the successful engagement of such individuals as a particular strength of the Even Start model. Such indicators are not easily captured by commonly used, large-grained measures.

Test Administration and Data Management: The Local Staff Perspective. Local program staff have a role in the national data collection and evaluation, most particularly in the third national evaluation. Local staff are often charged with collecting data on indicators of progress. Many view this data gathering with some resistance, seeing it as ill-suited for accurately capturing what they consider to be the real outcomes of their programs yet, at the same time, it grades or judges their work in ways that could affect their funding. In addition, discussions with local staff on the process of gathering and entering the required national data revealed multiple inter-pretations on the wording of various items and on respondents' answers. These factors influence local management of the data, and technical assis-tance may be insufficient to ensure consistent practice across sites (Ryan, Geissler, and Knell, 1996). This presents a significant concern, in that the national report stated that the variation in data quality across projects and evaluation years was significant to the degree that it impinged on the data usefulness at any level (U.S. Department of Education, 1998).

Data Analysis and Interpretation Across Diverse Programs. The programs themselves reflect considerable variation across implementation sites as well. As noted earlier, the funding for Even Start programs is designed to rely on an increasing percentage of local resources and eventu-ally become fully funded at the local level. Thus Even Start programs take on highly context-specific characteristics, evolving programmatically to fit the needs of their participants and the resources of that particular commu-nity. Although still employing the four core components of the model, pro-grams as implemented will necessarily look and operate quite differently in different settings.

Diversity is also evident in the local evaluations, as illustrated in a study conducted by Abt Associates (St. Pierre and Riccuti, 1998). To ascertain what information the local evaluations might contain that could be helpful outside their immediate application, the U.S. Department of Education con-tracted with Abt Associates to perform a review and synthesis of local eval-uations. A total of 125 local evaluations were collected; of those, 25 best evaluations were selected for review. One significant finding of this project was that the degree of diversity across sites regarding the evaluation ques-tions, design, methodology, and analysis was so great that virtually no design could be identified as "typical" local evaluation (St. Pierre and Ricciuti, 1998).

This variation among programs presents a problem in meaningfully interpreting the data collected nationally. As was the case in this instance, large-scale studies rely heavily on evaluation methods such as experimen-tal designs, standardized measurements, aggregate data, and statistical analysis—methods that remove contextual elements and describe an "aver-age" response (Bruner, 1994; Jacobs, 1988). The evaluators conducting the national study acknowledge that a weakness of such evaluations is that they are "based on data from individual projects that vary widely in the quality of implementation and in the activities implemented from project to proj-ect. . . . The evaluations *average* the results from sites that have taken different approaches to implementation" (St. Pierre, Layzer, and Barnes, 1995, p. 9; italics added). Such data aggregation may actually obscure evidence of significant and important effects and produce summary interpretations claiming little important effect (Brooks and Hayes, 1998).

In my opinion, local evaluators and state leadership believed that the national evaluation failed to accurately represent the conditions for program implementation, the diversity of programs, the diversity of program participants, and the diversity and subtlety of the outcomes of Even Start programs. With funding dependent on how the national evaluation would be viewed by policymakers, this perceived failure to capture and represent program impact could potentially undermine the future of the program.

Implications for Program Support. Local and state leadership recognized the real need to respond to the public call for accountability. Even Start had seen rapid expansion, from $14.8 million in appropriations in FY88 to $102 million in FY95, in the absence of data on outcomes. Instead, the increased funding was based largely on the logic of the theory underlying the approach. Into the late 1990s, it continued to find political support, despite the absence of strong evaluation findings (Vinovskis, 1999). Although Abt Associates and RMC Research Corp. have been candid about some of the methodological flaws of the national study, some political observers sensed that policymakers still see this as definitive scientific research (Vinovskis, 1999). They expressed concern that the absence of clearer indications of positive effect will ultimately influence appropriations negatively (Vinovskis, 1999). Indeed, while investment in Even Start was increasing in the early 1990s, the actual expenditure per family was declining from $6,000 per family in 1989 to $3,000 per family by 1998. During this same period, federal costs for Head Start increased from $2,900 to $4,600 per family (U.S. Department of Education, 1998).

Thus the absence of indication of substantive results presented a significant concern for local and state stakeholders. These concerns provided the impetus for the New York State Even Start Family Literacy Partnership.

Response from a State and Local Partnership

With over sixty programs in operation, New York State had more Even Start programs in place than any other state at the time of the second national evaluation (S. Henry, State Coordinator for Even Start Family Literacy Programs, New York State Department of Education, personal communication, 1998). Given that scope of implementation, New York had a considerable investment in the family literacy model. Concerned with the national evaluation's findings, officials with the New York State Education Department began a series of projects aimed at generating evaluations from multiple perspectives and using mixed methods to try to better define and reflect the program outcomes. Each of these evaluation projects involved partnerships among local Even Start program coordinators and the state office. This chapter highlights the efforts of one such project: the New York State Longitudinal Evaluation.

Initiated in 1997, this project involved a partnership between the State Education Department and seven local Even Start programs. Each of these programs had successfully completed a four-year funding cycle of service provision and had qualified to receive an additional four-year grant. Allocation of that grant was contingent on participation in the evaluation project.

These seven programs demonstrate the variations in model implementations across programs noted in the national report (U.S. Department of Education, 1998). For example, the four rural programs tend to be highly home-based early in the engagement process of service delivery. Participants are often quite isolated and frequently have a heavy—and sometimes negative—involvement with the human service system. This, coupled with a problematic personal history with public education, leaves participants experiencing a high level of distrust of educators and service providers. Conversely, the urban programs are often marked by a heavy emphasis on center-based services. Many participants in these programs are immigrants living in poverty who are highly literate in their own cultural reference but seek assistance in learning English as a second language.

The Longitudinal Evaluation Project used a participatory, collaborative approach. Officials from the State Education Department opted to work jointly with local stakeholders in selecting an evaluation method. This team included the local coordinators, the community-based partners, and evaluators for each of the seven programs. Representatives of two of the local programs provided project coordination, with resources and guidance from the State Education Department.

The team opted to complement the national evaluation effort by choosing a methodology that would permit the emergence of perspective through the lived experience of the program participants (Guba and Lincoln, 1989; Ryan, Geissler, and Knell, 1996; Stake, 1995). Such organic models for evaluation of family literacy programs find support in the literature, which emphasizes the need for methods more sensitive to the nuances of context (Bruner, 1994; Jacobs, 1988), with longitudinal studies (Hayes, 1996) and case studies (Brooks and Hayes, 1998) perhaps being particularly appropriate. Collaborative approaches to the evaluation of family literacy programs that enfranchise program practitioners and participants hold special promise (Hendrix, 1999–2000; Neuman, Caperelli, and Kee, 1998; Ryan, Geissler, and Knell, 1996). Noting the divergence of perspectives on effective family literacy practices and models, Neuman, Caperelli, and Kee (1998) point out that participants' perspectives of what program elements are most useful for them are largely absent from the literature. In addition, because of the variation in competencies, motives, environmental support, among others, across program participants, further study that maps out patterns among individuals served by family literacy programs would be useful for general programming, policymaking, and evaluation (Brooks and Hayes, 1998).

Operating from a similar set of values, the partnership elected to use a qualitative, participatory case study design to capture outcomes of the Even Start programs that might otherwise be missed by more externally determined, quantitatively oriented designs. The team sought to observe families participating in the program over time, documenting the course of their progress. Approaching the Longitudinal Project with this qualitative, participatory design provided an opportunity for local stakeholders to shape the direction of the data gathering, thereby allowing the stories to organically emerge.

Each program selected three families participating in services at that time and began a three-year data-gathering process. Families were purposively selected, with the sole criterion being that they had been in the program during the previous four-year cycle. Characteristics of the families selected were consistent with the majority of the participants in that program. The partnership intended to follow these families over the course of the three years and develop a portrait of each family and the role(s) that Even Start services played in their lives. The local evaluators, working together with local program staff, gathered data through interviews with families and other local stakeholders, engaged in participant observation, reviewed program records and documentation, and analyzed participants' writings.

Each program annually developed a detailed case study focusing primarily on one family and expanded on that case study in each subsequent year. The partnership met quarterly over the course of these four years. Partners reflected on the emerging portraits, generating additional questions and developing a core set of data elements that would be monitored across all case studies.

Several themes emerged across the family portraits developed through the Longitudinal Project. In particular, the case studies offered clear pictures of intergenerational poverty, accompanying low expectations for self, and the struggle with basic survival issues such as housing, transportation, and health care. The studies also revealed certain characteristics of services that influenced positive outcomes for families, highlighting the high level of energy required to achieve even modest gains in the face of such challenges (New York State Even Start Family Literacy Partnership, 2001).

Participant outcomes emerged that the team had not anticipated. For example, some of the case studies demonstrated that "graduation" from the program represented a fuzzy boundary. In fact, many participants continued to receive a small measure of service from the program while concurrently beginning to make active contributions toward it. Such contributions took many forms, including doing outreach, engaging new families, teaching or leading group sessions, and organizing new projects and activities for participants (New York State Even Start Family Literacy Partnership, 2001).

In essence, participants began to demonstrate a sense of ownership and pride in the program, as well as an enhanced sense of leadership with the immediate community. This is a profoundly striking shift, given the sense of isolation and alienation many participants experienced prior to engagement in the service. The shift also has implications for program design and implementation. As such, it represents an outcome of note for programs and local stakeholders. Yet it is one outcome that could not have been captured by the national study.

Lessons Learned from the State and Local Collaborative Evaluation Project

The project has just begun to use this work to lobby for a shift in understanding and evaluating the effects of the Even Start programs. However, both the process and products of this work are already influencing the way in which evaluation of Even Start is being conducted in New York State.

Evaluation lessons learned from this project include the finding that participation in the process of the longitudinal evaluation project involved opportunity for sharing and reflection on the work of the projects, as well as on the process of evaluation itself (New York State Even Start Family Literacy Partnership, 2001). The team negotiated the core elements of each family portrait to best reflect the stories of the participants, given the variation among participants and contexts. Participants found that this process enhanced the quality of the evaluation product. Many participants also found this dialogue raised the bar for the programs, providing insights into ways in which programs could be strengthened. The process thus illustrates the learning that can occur through collaborative evaluation (Neuman, 1998; New York State Even Start Family Literacy Partnership, 2001; Ryan, Geissler, and Knell, 1996).

Another lesson was that involvement in the longitudinal evaluation affected how some of the local direct program staff saw evaluation and what it could contribute. Many developed an appreciation for evaluation, seeing how it could help them view and understand the impact of the program in new ways. In this instance, appreciation came through learning about the lived experiences of participants and the meaning the various program components held for these families (New York State Even Start Family Literacy Partnership, 2001). Many saw this as evaluation that was relevant to them, offering them clear insight into how programs might be strengthened.

A third lesson: the family portraits provided an accessible vehicle for communicating to other stakeholders the meaning that Even Start had for participating families. The case studies were readily understandable, in particular for local stakeholders such as community members and school personnel (New York State Even Start Family Literacy Partnership, 2001). In this way, the case studies helped to build local support for and ownership of the program, which is one of the overarching goals of the legislation for Even Start.

And finally, offshoots of this project have been numerous, and they reflect an enhanced sense of capacity for proactively advancing the field of family literacy. For example, the case studies are being used in professional development of staff and orientation for new programs. Members of the Longitudinal Team have also analyzed the case studies to identify the benchmarks of family progress. Recent federal authorization requires all states to develop program performance indicators (U.S. Department of Education, 1998). The New York State Education Department, in conjunction with local programs, is using these benchmarks of family progress to inform the indicators it is developing in accordance with federal regulations. Another longitudinal project, with a new set of local Even Start programs, has been launched to study a new set of questions. Furthermore, the New York state and local partnership is using the case studies to educate others at the regional and national levels. They have published the case studies and have made presentations on this work at relevant national conferences. Through these activities, the partnership of state and local stakeholders seeks to use evaluation to influence the policy agenda.

Discussion

As this example illustrates, the perspective each governmental level brings to viewing social programs varies as a function of its own context, intended audience, and role. The context for the national study is the federal policy-making arena. This audience seeks scientifically supported evidence to attest to the efficacy of a model being implemented across the nation to assure that federal dollars are being wisely spent. Here the primary question—What are the long-term effects of program participation?—is conceptualized and approached through the lens of the intended outcomes (Nickse, 1993).

Conversely, the intended aim of the local evaluations is to inform local stakeholders about program improvement. Local evaluation provides a closer focus to the measurement of short-term objectives, with the guiding question being, How can we do a better job serving our participants? (Jacobs, 1988). At the local level, evaluation questions would be conceptualized and approached from a perspective that would be most useful to local stakeholders.

The evaluation design selected at different levels reflects these different perspectives and different questions (Ryan, Geissler, and Knell, 1996). In this instance, the national study selected the experimental design for its ability to inform across the large scale and its credibility with the policy audience. Local evaluations vary considerably in order to be responsive to the needs of the local stakeholders. Generally, however, evaluation efforts at these two levels are construed as separate activities, with the local efforts to inform only the local stakeholders and national effort being geared toward informing policymakers of the overall impact of the model.

State agencies are in an intermediary role, ensuring local compliance with federal mandate yet also noting points of dissonance with the local perspective and practical experience and seeking to communicate that to the national audiences—in particular, to those with policymaking influence and authority.

As this case illustrates, however, perspectives can emerge from local programs that highlight the limitations of such large-scale studies. Response to the authorizing mandate, using the best designs available, does not ensure adequate representation of program effects. Faced with that, a state and local collaboration sought to use a collaboratively designed, qualitative inquiry to influence the policy agenda by broadening understanding of the program. I wish to draw attention to four observations in light of this effort.

First, this case example of evaluation use challenges the conceptualization of local government's function as limited to passively implementing policy determined at higher government levels and implementing evaluation solely for the purpose of informing local stakeholders. Rather, the case portrays local-level officials as actors, not reactors, learning from program implementation and evaluation and seeking to use evaluation to correct what they see as inaccuracies in national-level evaluation.

Second, this case example highlights some of the challenges for evaluating complex social programs. The case portrays the challenge of understanding, assessing, and representing progress and growth across widely varying participants and contexts, as well as when that growth varies with each individual family's needs, goals, and pace (Bruner, 1994). The case also redefines the challenge of determining how to systematize this measurement of progress and the program's role in fostering that progress so that decision making is informed at the national level. This illustration suggests the potential for a mixed-method approach, integrating the perspectives of multiple stakeholders from all levels of the intergovernmental context to frame evaluation objectives, criteria, and constructs for summative national evaluation.

Third, the case example also highlights the role of stakeholder involvement in evaluation design and its connection to evaluation use. Not only did the national evaluations fail to capture all desired program outcomes but the national evaluation process also missed an important opportunity to play a key role in developing the capacity of local program staff and administrators. The experience both within the participating programs and across the family literacy programs in New York State suggests that collaborative evaluation can have a meaningful impact on those engaged in the process, enhancing the learning acquired in ways that strengthen programs across a regional and state level.

And finally, this case expands the nature of the questions for evaluation and research, suggesting these questions instead:

What are the characteristics of the various subgroups within the general population that participate in social programs?

What kinds of outcomes can be anticipated for these different subgroups? Under what conditions does a particular model produce positive outcomes? Given the need for social programs to adapt to local conditions, in what ways can the authorizing environment support sound development and local integration of these programs? What role might evaluation play in such an effort?

Conclusion

The current movement is toward encouraging and implementing family support that is integrated, holistic, and individualized rather than toward teaching a specific set of skills to correct an externally determined deficit. Such integrated and individualized programming presents significant challenges to evaluation. The New York Longitudinal Evaluation Project illustrates the potential for collaboratively generated case studies to both illuminate the subtleties of the human experience in unique contexts and identify the commonalties that support success.

References

Brooks, G., and Hayes, A. *Issues in Evaluating Family Literacy Programs in Britain and the United States.* Louisville, Ky.: National Center for Family Literacy, 1998.

Bruner, C. "A Framework for Measuring the Potential for Comprehensive Service Strategies." In N. Young, S. Gardner, S. Coley, L. Schorr, and C. Bruner, *Making a Difference: Moving to Outcome-Based Accountability for Comprehensive Service Reforms.* Des Moines, Iowa: National Center for Service Integration, 1994.

Guba, E., and Lincoln, Y. *Fourth Generation Evaluation.* Thousand Oaks, Calif.: Sage, 1989.

Hayes, A. "Longitudinal Study of Family Literacy Program Outcomes." In L. A. Benjamin and J. Lord (eds.), *Summary and Papers of a National Symposium.* Washington, D.C.: U.S. Department of Education, 1996. Accessible at http://www.gov/pubs/FamLit/long.html.

Hendrix, S. "Family Literacy Education: Panacea or False Promise?" *Journal of Adolescent and Adult Literacy,* 1999–2000, *43,* 338–346.

Jacobs, F. H. "The Five-Tiered Approach to Evaluation: Context and Implementation." In H. B. Weiss and F. H. Jacobs (eds.), *Evaluating Family Programs.* Hawthorne, N.Y.: Aldine De Gruyter, 1988.

Morrow, L. M., Tracey, D. H., and Maxwell, C. M. (eds.). *A Survey of Family Literacy.* Newark, Del.: International Reading Association, 1995.

Neuman, S., Caperelli, B., and Kee, C. "Literacy Learning, a Family Matter." *The Reading Teacher,* 1998, *52,* 244–252.

New York State Even Start Family Literacy Partnership, *Portraits of Families: The Longitudinal Evaluation Project 1997–2001,* Albany, N.Y.: New York State Education Department, 2001.

Nickse, R. *A Typology of Family and Intergenerational Literacy Programs: Implications for Evaluation,* 1993, *15,* 76–93. (ED 362 766)

Ryan, K. E., Geissler, B., and Knell, S. "Evaluating Family Literacy Programs: Tales from the Field." In D. K. Dickinson, *Bridges to Literacy: Children, Families and Schools,* Cambridge, Mass.: Blackwell Publishers, 1994.

Ryan, K. E., Geissler, B., and Knell, S. "Progress and Accountability in Family Literacy: Lessons from a Collaborative Approach." *Education and Program Planning*, 1996, *19*(3), 263–272.

Stake, R. *The Art of Case Study Research.* Thousand Oaks, Calif.: Sage, 1995.

St. Pierre, R. G., Layzer, J. I., and Barnes, H. V. "Two-Generation Programs: Design, Cost and Short-Term Effectiveness." *The Future of Children*, 1995, *5*(3), 76–93. Accessible at http://www.futureofchildren.org/1to/04

St. Pierre, R. G., and Ricciuti, A. *Synthesis of State and Local Even Start Evaluations.* Cambridge Mass.: Abt Associates, 1998.

St. Pierre, R. G., Ricciuti, A., and Tao, F. *Third National Even Start Evaluation: Overview.* Washington, D.C.: U.S. Department of Education, Planning and Evaluation, 1997.

St. Pierre, R. G., Swartz, J., Gamse, B., Murray, S., Deck, D., and Nickel, P. *National Evaluation of the Even Start Family Literacy Program: Final Report.* Cambridge, Mass.: Abt Associates' Report, U.S. Department of Education, Planning and Evaluation Service, 1995.

St. Pierre, R. G., Swartz, J., Murray, S., and Deck, D. *Improving Family Literacy: Findings from the National Even Start Evaluation.* Cambridge, Mass: Abt Associates, 1996.

Tao, F., Schwartz, J., St. Pierre, R. G., and Tarr, H. *National Evaluation of the Even Start Family Literacy Program: 1995 Interim Report.* Washington, D.C.: U.S. Department of Education, Planning and Evaluation Service, 1997.

U.S. Department of Education. *Even Start: Evidence from the Past and a Look to the Future.* Washington, D.C.: U.S. Department of Education, Planning and Evaluation Services, 1998.

Vinovskis, M. *History and Educational Policymaking,* New Haven, Conn.: Yale University Press, 1999.

SUSAN BOSER is assistant professor of sociology at Indiana University of Pennsylvania and coordinator of the doctoral program for administrative and leadership studies. As a local evaluator for Even Start programs in upstate New York between 1997 and 2000, she contributed to the New York Longitudinal Evaluation.

This chapter presents a state agency's approach to developing and improving the self-assessment and accountability of local programs overseen and funded by a large statewide program. Specifically, a self-assessment approach to evaluating local tobacco control programs and projects in California is introduced as an example of "empowerment evaluation" in action.

Building Local Program Evaluation Capacity Toward a Comprehensive Evaluation

Hao Tang, David W. Cowling, Kristi Koumjian, April Roeseler, Jon Lloyd, Todd Rogers

It is common in a government setting that agencies at different levels (federal, state, and local), with the help of outside stakeholders, work together to accomplish the goal of a given program. The complexity of the relationships within these settings frequently complicates and may hamper program implementation and evaluation. Misunderstandings or perceptions of mistreatment can damage relationships between the state and local agencies, the local agency and the coalition, the coalition and the community, and the community and the state agency, with the result that program momentum is lost and public funds are wasted. However, a thorough understanding of the needs of the agencies involved, paired with guidance or technical assistance on request, can lay the groundwork for harmonious relationships. Such relationships, in turn, can maximize efficient program implementation and benefits.

Empowerment evaluation (Fetterman, 1994a; Fetterman, 1996) is one innovative approach that recognizes the importance of multichannel relationships existing in governmental settings and other interagency settings; it provides a valuable theoretical framework for understanding and solving many of the challenges associated with program evaluation. The California Department of Health Services Tobacco Control Program (TCP) made decisions based on concepts that, in retrospect, were consistent with those used in empowerment evaluation. Subsequently, TCP staff intentionally used this approach to local program evaluation as a means to achieve maximum local

NEW DIRECTIONS FOR EVALUATION, no. 95, Fall 2002 © Wiley Periodicals, Inc.

program effectiveness. Concepts of empowerment evaluation were gradually incorporated and are now used explicitly to achieve local program accountability to the state as well. Thus empowerment evaluation has become fundamental to fulfilling the extremely ambitious statutory mandate for the evaluation of California's comprehensive TCP.

Empowerment Evaluation: A Self-Assessment Approach

Empowerment evaluation was first introduced by Fetterman in 1994 (Fetterman, 1994a). He described *empowerment evaluation* as "the use of evaluation concepts, techniques, and findings to foster improvement and self-determination" (Fetterman, 1996). The major focus of the approach is "to help people help themselves and improve their programs using a form of self-evaluation and reflection" (Fetterman, 1996, p. 4). Fetterman's conception, derived from Zimmerman's work on empowerment theory, emphasized that the empowering process "helps people develop skills so they can become independent problem solvers and decision makers" (Zimmerman, 2000, p. 46).

Four major steps can be identified in empowerment evaluation: (1) taking stock or self-rating the state of the program, (2) setting goals that illustrate potential improvements of the program in the future, (3) developing strategies to meet the goals, and (4) documenting progress by monitoring the program (Fetterman, 1994b). From the practitioner's point of view, these major steps do not conflict with or overturn "traditional evaluation" processes such as formative research, process evaluation or monitoring, or impact assessment (Shadish, Cook, and Leviton, 1991; Rossi, Freeman, and Lipsey, 1999).

The main distinction between empowerment evaluation and traditional evaluation involves identifying the party or parties responsible for taking the four steps identified earlier. In traditional evaluation, most of the evaluation work is conducted by independent evaluators. However, in empowerment evaluation, program staff members, collaborating with outside evaluators, perform a self-assessment.

In addition to the four steps of empowerment evaluation, Fetterman recognized five facets of it, including *training, facilitation, advocacy, illumination,* and *liberation* (Fetterman, 1996). It is in these five facets that the distinction between traditional evaluation and empowerment evaluation can be seen. *Training* and *facilitation* refer respectively to teaching and to helping program staff conduct their own evaluations. Programmatic needs that can be identified during the evaluation process may result in advocacy for the program by an evaluator. Through a brainstorming session with help from outside evaluators, program staff members develop *illumination,* or a clearer understanding of the role and array of potential benefits of program evaluation. This success may lead to *liberation,* based on the thorough understanding of program evaluation that results from a self-learning process with some coaching and help from outside evaluators.

In the following text, we use the experience of the California TCP in local program evaluation as a case study to illustrate the utility and feasibility of empowerment evaluation in a comprehensive state-funded program. In the conclusion, we depict how the results of local program evaluations can serve as an integral part of a comprehensive evaluation for the state program. Like other conceptual frameworks in evaluation, empowerment evaluation is neither a doctrinal theory nor a practice guide. Over time, TCP has gradually added more empowerment evaluation concepts in its approach to local program evaluation and has made adjustments to accommodate the reality of conducting evaluations in a complex authorizing environment—an issue that many other state programs face.

Authorizing Environment

California was the first state to establish a large-scale anti-tobacco health education program funded by tobacco tax revenues (California Tobacco Tax and Health Promotion Act of 1988, Proposition 99). The California Department of Health Services has operated a $60–$80 million-per-year TCP since 1989. The California TCP is a comprehensive health education program that uses a "social norm change" approach, aimed at reducing both tobacco use and the exposure to secondhand tobacco smoke, which, in combination, have been found to cause the premature deaths of more than 400,000 Americans each year (Malarcher and others, 2000). TCP supports sixty-one local health department programs, more than one hundred local, regional, and statewide competitive grant projects, a statewide media campaign, and an extensive surveillance and evaluation effort.

California's TCP has a legislative mandate to evaluate the effectiveness of the programs implemented at the local level. Specifically, the California Health and Safety Code §104375 states, "The department shall. . . . evaluate the department's local and state tobacco control programs under this article" (California Health and Safety Code §104375, 1996). As a part of the mandate, TCP is held accountable for the use of funds by various governmental bodies, public constituency groups, and third-party organizations such as the tobacco industry.

Challenges. During the past twelve years, TCP has gone through some turbulent periods when outside forces sought to discredit the program. These detractors have included several legislators, tobacco industry front groups, lobbyists, and agencies or persons who failed to receive funding from competitive grant procurements. One strategy used by those seeking to discredit the program was to identify specific local programs that were perceived as ineffective by the public and had been overtly aggressive toward the tobacco industry. Program opponents brandished such examples to attack the program during both the reauthorization of TCP and during budget hearings. Some major challenges are identified as follows:

- California's TCP was the first well-funded, comprehensive effort of its kind in the nation. As such, the program provided both an opportunity and a responsibility to demonstrate the effectiveness of a comprehensive TCP. This responsibility was taken seriously because it was understood that if California's TCP failed, other states would not appropriate resources for similar programs.
- The enabling legislation for TCP imposed rigorous evaluation requirements and timelines for the completion of baseline surveillance activities. The requirement for an independent evaluation also established the need to compare effectiveness of various interventions, which strained the capacity of state government to be responsive.
- Taking advantage of the complexity of the TCP authorizing environment, the tobacco industry exerted considerable direct and indirect negative pressure on the program. The industry attempted to defeat the initiative that established the program, to eliminate the media campaign, and to reduce funding for the local programs once those had begun.
- There was a high level of ownership among the voluntary health organizations that had committed human and financial resources to secure funding for TCP. Maintaining their support and satisfaction with the operation and outcomes of TCP was critical. The importance of this support subsequently was put to the test when funding for TCP was redirected toward the provision of medical care services. When the funding was redirected, voluntary health organizations sued the state. As a result of the suit, funding for media campaign, local tobacco control, and evaluation programs was restored.

Responses. TCP staff quickly realized the importance of responding to the challenges under this authorizing environment by improving their evaluation efforts. However, the evaluation mandate not only allowed TCP to justify its existence with evidence but drove funding priorities in terms of local program strategies that deserved to be widely disseminated and continuously funded.

Over the years, TCP has taken steps to establish and strengthen both the surveillance and evaluation components of local programs and has conducted several special evaluation projects throughout the year. The surveillance system includes several large-scale telephone surveys of adults and youths. These surveys collect information on tobacco use, secondhand smoke exposure, exposure to tobacco marketing, and attitudes about tobacco industry practices and tobacco control policies.

In 2000, two additional surveys were added to the existing surveillance system. These were a Media Tracking Study and a California Student

Tobacco Survey. The Media Tracking Survey collects information on tobacco use, secondhand smoke exposure, and attitudes related to tobacco, as well as extensive information on exposure to anti-tobacco-use advertising and to pro-tobacco-use advertising. Information is collected from adults in California, as well as in the rest of the United States, to better understand the impact of California's extensive anti-tobacco-use media campaign. The California Student Tobacco Survey includes a student survey, a principal survey, and a Tobacco Use Prevention Educator survey. This survey assesses tobacco use, secondhand smoke exposure, exposure to TCP and the nature of school-based anti-tobacco-use curricula, and compliance with school campus smoke-free requirements. Results from the California Student Tobacco Survey will be comparable to the Youth Tobacco Survey that is conducted nationally.

Compared to the stable surveillance mechanisms and special statewide evaluation projects that have been carried out, local program evaluation has had a more checkered history and has undergone a substantial evolution over the course of the past decade. Changes to TCP's approach to local program evaluation reflect a growing awareness that integration of a self-assessment approach produces better planned, more effective, and more accountable interventions, which are critical to the success of the overall program.

TCP evolved through three stages to empower local programs with proper resources and requirements to conduct self-evaluations. In the first two stages, TCP searched for an effective approach to improve local program evaluation from its own experiences because there were no known successful exemplars to emulate (that is, a large-scale, multilevel, and multisite program in a complex authorizing environment). It was not until the third stage that TCP formally introduced the concept of empowerment evaluation to local program evaluation practice.

Stage One: Evolution of Local Program Evaluation

The first stage occurred prior to 1996, when local programs were evaluated using tracking studies by an independent research organization. These fairly traditional tracking studies required local projects to complete thirteen different standardized forms on a monthly basis. Although this evaluation provided a broad picture of the local programs, one major shortcoming was that the measures used by the independent evaluators were not able to address the diversity of interventions employed by the approximately two hundred local projects. Another was that the evaluation forms were burdensome to local projects. A natural consequence of inadequate measures, combined with burdensome collection methods, was that the evaluation results did not adequately describe the effectiveness or performance of individual local programs, which were highly diversified. Inadequate descriptions, in turn, inherently compromised the independent evaluators' ability to reach conclusions about the impact of the local programs. For example, local health departments served populations ranging in size from twelve hundred to 9 million. The TCP budget allocation for these counties ranged from $150,000 to over $4.7 million annually. State agency staff began to question whether a comprehensive evaluation of the diversified local health departments and competitive grantees might be beyond the capacity of any one research group.

Early in the implementation of TCP, the state agency staff recommended that local programs use 10 percent of their funds for evaluation purposes. Due to a combination of lack of assertive leadership from TCP, poor planning and organization, and a lack of priority, fewer than 1 percent of projects were responsive to this recommendation. Beginning in 1994, local programs were required to select at least one intervention for extensive self-evaluation, which would describe data collection activities, report writing, and dissemination efforts. However, no standard protocol was available for local program staff to follow. Thus process data, including case studies, were the most common forms of evaluation information submitted to the state during this period.

Stage Two: Steps Toward Empowerment Evaluation

During Stage One, state TCP staff began to recognize the need for clear and established minimum requirements and standards for evaluating local program effectiveness to promote better local program evaluation.

Ten Percent Solution. Recognition of the need for minimum standard requirements led to the second stage, which began in 1996. The first requirement for a Local Program Evaluation (LPE) Initiative was formally established, and it included a "10 percent solution." The 10 percent solution required all locally funded agencies to allocate at least 10 percent of their budgets toward program evaluation and to have a qualified evaluator (local program evaluator) assist with development and implementation of their evaluation plans. Local program evaluators could be either hired externally or be on staff, provided the individual had experience in evaluation and research.

Evaluation Plan: A Standard Format. An additional requirement of the second stage was that local programs were required to describe their evaluation plans in a standard format as part of their contract work plans. Evaluation plans were to incorporate appropriate process evaluation measures and outcome evaluation strategies.

Evaluation Report: Tell Your Story. A third requirement of the second stage of local program evaluation was that local programs produce a final evaluation report for each of their objectives. Final evaluation reports included both outcome and process data and described the relationship between each objective and its observed outcomes. The evaluation reports included a cover page, an abstract, description of the project and evaluation methods, presentation of the results, and discussion and recommendations sections. These reports were abstracted, summarized, and maintained in a local program evaluation database. Since 1996, all of these requirements were included in all local program contracts.

Facilitation of Training and Assistance. In response to the new requirements of the second stage of local program evaluation, the local program staff reacted with considerable apprehension and displeasure. State TCP staff had to convince them that the purpose of the evaluation was not to discredit them but to improve and showcase their projects' effectiveness. A joint workgroup of local project directors and evaluators was created to facilitate implementation of the requirements and to help design trainings and develop evaluation tools. Two publications produced to aid local programs and their evaluators in completing final evaluation reports were *Using Case Studies to Do Program Evaluation* (Edith, 1999) and *Guidelines for Preparing an Evaluation Report* (Albright, Howard-Pitney, Roberts, and Zicarelli, 1998).

With the increase in both evaluation requirements and technical assistance, more rigorous contract monitoring was employed to ensure the progress of local program evaluations. Although contract payment was suspended if a local project did not meet the minimum evaluation requirements, it was made clear to local program staff that they would not be penalized for failure to achieve their objectives. Evaluation results would neither affect current funding nor eligibility for future funding.

Problems After the Second Stage. The combination of establishing evaluation requirements and providing resources during the second stage of local program evaluation resulted in a big step forward for local program staff. Many began to fully appreciate the importance of evaluation, not only to enhance their programs' efficiency but to demonstrate accountability. Local program staff were encouraged to submit abstracts for inclusion in a showcase—the TCP "Compendium of Abstracts" (California Department of Health Services, 1999)—produced by the state TCP. Creating this showcase allowed the local program staff's work to be recognized by others in their field and, as such, identified as one of the illumination efforts intrinsic to empowerment evaluation.

Although the quality of many local programs improved during the first and second stages, some common and serious problems remained, including an imbalance of budget allocations for evaluation across the different sizes of local programs in the state, a lack of systematic or scientific evaluation design, and a disconnection between local evaluation and statewide evaluation efforts.

The requirement for a 10 percent budget allocation toward evaluation was difficult for most local programs to fulfill. Local program staff often had to spend time and energy allocating resources to evaluate objectives in ways that did not necessarily correspond to program priorities. In other words, the requirement actually diluted the funds earmarked for the most critical evaluation activities. To correct this problem, TCP worked closely with the local program staff to identify at least three objectives that would be the focus of a more in-depth evaluation and would therefore receive the bulk of the resources earmarked for evaluation activities.

In general, the efforts from TCP in the second stage formed the basis for the type of empowerment evaluation that would be more fully conceptualized and developed in the third stage. During the second stage, TCP staff did not apply the concept of empowerment evaluation in local program evaluation. However, some strategies that are employed by empowerment evaluation such as training, facilitation, advocacy, and even illumination were unconsciously adopted, based on the feedback from local program staff.

Stage Three: Empowerment Evaluation at Work

Given the problems associated with Stage Two, TCP staff clearly realized that further improvements were needed to fulfill the legislative mandate for evaluation, which suggested using "elements of controlled experimental methods" to determine "the comparative effectiveness of individual program designs that shall be used in funding decisions and program modifications"(California Health and Safety Code §104375, 1996, p. 174). The opportunity for a new stage came in 2000, when TCP introduced a community planning model called Communities of Excellence, which explicitly incorporated empowerment evaluation to assist local program staff in preparing their new three-year tobacco control plans. The complete empowerment evaluation process is depicted in Figure 3.1.

Self-Assessment Using Communities of Excellence Indicators and Assets. Communities can achieve excellence by involving a motivated and diverse group of people to assess where they are now and where they need to be. Through the Communities of Excellence model, local program staff and coalition members are systematically assessing their communities in relation to standardized indicators and assets relevant to tobacco control. Based on their findings, the local program staff and community members make decisions about future objectives, interventions, and evaluation plans. Performing these community assessments is the "taking stock" step specified in the empowerment evaluation process (Fetterman, 1994b).

Setting Objectives Based on Assessment Results. Within TCP's four program priority areas, Communities of Excellence identified sixty-three community indicators that cover almost all areas of tobacco control activities. Thirteen of the indicators are designated as core indicators based on perceived assessment quality and feasibility (see Table 3.1).

Local programs have been required to assess the thirteen core indicators and to select three additional, noncore indicators for attention. Based on their assessments, local program staff decide which indicators or areas need to be addressed in their communities. Local programs are required to furnish

Figure 3.1. The Process of Empowerment Evaluation for Local TCP

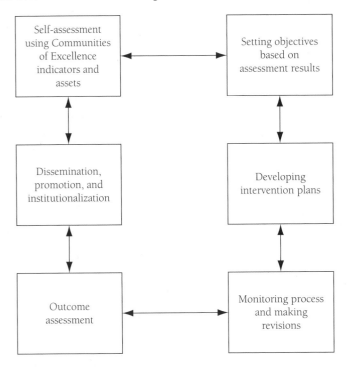

measurable objectives addressing the indicators selected and to identify at least three of the objectives as primary; these are subject to a more thorough and systematic evaluation than the others. Two of the three primary objectives have to be tied to core indicators. In the Communities of Excellence model, at least one sample objective is provided for each core and each non-core indicator. These requirements and examples help local program staff set workable and measurable objectives that are tied to local priorities, which equates to the "goal setting" step in the empowerment evaluation model (Fetterman, 1994b) and serves to maximize their budgets in a way that is thoughtfully aligned to their priorities.

Developing Intervention Plans, Monitoring Process, Making Revisions, and Assessing Outcome. Along with Communities of Excellence came a new reporting system for local health departments. The local health departments began entering their work plans into a Web-based system called the Online Tobacco Information System (OTIS). OTIS was designed to standardize and streamline program, evaluation, and budget data collection. Even though some flexibility is lost, the standardization of information collection provides state TCP staff with the ability to better monitor the contracts, evaluations, and budgets of the local programs. A

Table 3.1.   Core Community Indicators

Priority Area	Subcategory	Core Indicator
Counter pro-tobacco influences	Marketing and deglamorization	Extent of in-store tobacco advertising and promotions or the proportion of communities with policies that control the extent of in-store tobacco advertising and promotions Extent of tobacco advertising outside retail stores or the proportion of communities with policies that control the extent of tobacco advertising outside retail stores Extent of tobacco sponsorship at public (for example, county fairs) and private events (for example, concerts, bars) or the proportion of entertainment and sporting venues with policies that regulate tobacco sponsorship
	School-based prevention indicators	Proportion of schools that provide intensive tobacco use prevention instruction in junior high and middle school years, with reinforcement in high school using a curriculum that provides instruction on the negative physiological and social consequences of tobacco use, social influences on tobacco use, peer norms regarding tobacco use, and refusal skills (Centers for Disease Control Guideline)
Reduce exposure to secondhand smoke	Indicators of reduction of exposure to secondhand smoke	Extent of enforcement and compliance of state and local smoke-free bar and gaming laws Extent of compliance with state law that prohibits the use of tobacco by all students, school staff, parents, and visitors in public school district-owned or leased buildings, on district grounds, and in district vehicles Proportion of homes with a smoker in the household that report a smoke-free home Extent of outdoor recreational facilities (for example, fairgrounds, amusement parks, playgrounds, sport stadiums) that have policies designating a portion or all outdoor areas as smoke-free
Reduce the availability of tobacco	Indicators of reduction of tobacco availability	Extent of compliance with state laws prohibiting tobacco sales to minors and requiring ID checks Proportion of communities with tobacco retail licensing Proportion of communities that control self-service sales of tobacco
Promote tobacco cessation services	Indication of cessation services promotion	Extent of the availability and use of culturally and linguistically appropriate behavior-modification-based tobacco cessation services in the community Extent of public school districts that provide cessation support for students and all staff who use tobacco (Centers for Disease Control Guidelines)

goal of OTIS is to obtain information that allows state TCP staff to more effectively modify and improve programmatic efforts.

Each objective submitted by local programs requires both an intervention plan and an evaluation plan. OTIS collects information about the plans in a systematic fashion and has two organizing tracks. One track focuses on objectives related to policy adoption, which is considered a process objective. The second track relates to outcome objectives, which focus on (1) changing individual behavior, (2) changing attitudes or beliefs, and (3) enforcing existing policies.

The information collected in evaluation plans for policy adoption objectives includes

- The process evaluation activities that are to be conducted (focus groups, key opinion leader surveys, public opinion surveys, and so on)
- The timing of process activities to be conducted and completed
- The methods for dissemination of evaluation results
- The limitations of or challenges to the evaluation plans

The evaluation plan information intended to address nonpolicy objectives is much more comprehensive due to the nature of these anticipated outcomes. For example, local programs must answer questions regarding the outcomes being measured, the general evaluation design (experimental, quasi-experimental, nonexperimental), specifics of the evaluation design, the types of analysis to be performed, and the methods for disseminating evaluation results. In addition, several questions are asked in order to determine the timelines for evaluation activities.

The goal of data collection in OTIS was not only to provide information for the oversight of the contracts by state TCP staff but to allow for an examination of the range of evaluation efforts across the state. For example, we would expect few objectives to use experimental designs due to cost and effort; however, over time we hope to see an increase in the proportion of objectives using quasi-experimental designs versus nonexperimental designs, especially for specific types of objectives or indicators. Preliminary data show that 11 objectives will be evaluated using an experimental design, 65 will use a quasi-experimental study design, and 230 will use a nonexperimental design. In reviewing how the data will be collected for the outcome objectives, 22 projects have indicated that they will use face-to-face surveys, 35 will use telephone surveys, 45 will use written surveys, and 128 will conduct observation surveys. For the formative-process objectives, 45 projects will use focus groups, 120 will use a key opinion leader survey, 49 will use a public opinion poll, and 35 will collect data from city council records. TCP will be able to generate reports from the database on the variety of other variables collected to help guide local program evaluation in the future.

After contracts were initiated, OTIS provided similar tracking forms for progress reports. Local program staff entered the information describing the intervention and evaluation activities that were conducted during the report period—for example, baseline surveys. A final evaluation report was required to document any outcome results. With the addition of OTIS and Communities of Excellence and because of the new and more stringent evaluation requirements adopted during the third stage, local program staff were provided with two additional resources, one in print and the other in human resources. State TCP staff understood that more rigorous requirements paired with more sophisticated models meant that local program staff would need more support, not only in writing their evaluation plans but in understanding the value of having high-quality evaluation plans.

The state TCP prepared a printed resource titled "Local Program Evaluation Planning Guide" (Tang, Koumjian, Cowling, and Roeseler, 2001) to enhance local staff independence. The guide could also be used in conjunction with the Communities of Excellence model. The content and flexibility were designed to help local program staff plan the evaluation of interventions that address objectives written around the thirteen core indicators. The guide provided samples of objectives and evaluation plans addressing each of the thirteen core indicators. Detailed information included the type of study design that should be used, how the sample should be selected, where the data should be collected, and how the data should be analyzed, along with ideas about disseminating results. In addition to sample objectives and evaluation plans, the guide provided local program staff with the following: a list of over thirty definitions relevant to evaluation, tips and examples of how to use the guide, a list of sample activities for each objective, and an appendix that contains over twenty sample survey instruments that local programs are highly encouraged to use.

Although the "Local Program Evaluation Planning Guide" only provided examples for the thirteen core indicators, evaluation plans may be easily adapted to fit any objective in the local programs work plans. This unique and resourceful "evaluation cookbook" made it easier for local program staff to correctly use standardized program evaluation practices with a minimum of stress.

A second resource instituted in this new stage was the creation of technical assistant consultant positions. TCP contracted with seven technical assistant consultants to provide technical assistance or coaching to local health department staff on program evaluation tasks. These consultants are from academia and have extensive knowledge in the areas of evaluation and tobacco control. During the first year, each consultant was on contract for ninety hours, and each was assigned to work with several local health departments.

After being assigned to local programs, the consultants attended a two-day technical-assistance meeting with local program staff. The consultants participated in one-on-one consultations and in roundtable discussions on various issues in tobacco control. During these meetings, local program staff had opportunities to seek expert advice on their evaluation plans and to receive preliminary feedback on their work in progress. After attending the two-day technical assistance meetings, local program staff submitted their final work plans to TCP. The consultants then participated in an in-house review of their assigned programs' plans. During this review, the consultants provided extensive comments and feedback on program evaluation plans, making suggestions for change and monitoring the progress of the plans after the meetings.

After the work plan submission, two technical assistant consultants conducted a workshop for local project directors and local program evaluators. Workshop content was determined by the consultants' experiences in coaching evaluators during the planning stage and by their vision of future program needs. Thus they focused on how to better document evaluation progress, especially on how to fine-tune the work plan based on process information and on how to monitor the intervention plan effectively.

The technical assistant consultants' contracts have since been extended to include an additional ninety hours of work to be done during 2002 and 2003. In addition to providing ongoing technical assistance to each of their assigned programs, the consultants are expected to aid local program staff in completing final evaluation reports. Local programs still must set aside 10 percent of their budgets for evaluation, but under Phase Three they have more direct support for evaluation from the technical assistant consultant system.

Disseminating, Promoting, and Institutionalizing. Reports about the outcomes of local program evaluations were to be disseminated through channels identified in the local program's work plan. Even before the introduction of Communities of Excellence and OTIS, local program staff realized that outcome evaluation results could be presented as convincing messages relating to tobacco control that could easily be used by media outlets. The results also lent themselves to identifying "best practices" in the tobacco control field. Institutionalization and documentation of evaluation results is setting the stage for the first step of a new three-year empowerment evaluation process and work plan. New self-assessments are to be prepared using Communities of Excellence indicators. Thus, as the current cycle is completed, a new cycle can start in an orderly and systematic manner.

Toward a Comprehensive Evaluation

One of the most important goals of the third evaluation phase was to produce comparable local program evaluation results that would enable TCP, as well as outside researchers, to conduct analyses using community evaluation data. The analyses were intended to provide more insights and capture a "big picture" when regional program evaluation data and statewide surveillance data were integrated. It is believed that empowerment of local programs with self-evaluations based on sound scientific principles is the best strategy to achieving the statutory mandate "to direct the most efficient allocation of resources. . . . to accomplish the maximum prevention and reduction of tobacco use" (California Health and Safety Code §104375, 1996, p. 174).

Tying the local program evaluations to the overall evaluation of TCP in California has been and will continue to be difficult because of the sheer number of local programs (approximately two hundred) and their diversity. Previous attempts at evaluating the overall and individual effects of programs (media, local program, and school) have shown that a comprehensive program is most effective, but these attempts have been unable to draw definitive conclusions about which pieces are the most influential (The Gallup Organization, 2000). The current framework for evaluation is less suited to making sweeping conclusions and instead examines local programs individually to determine whether any impact of their interventions can be observed. The decision to concentrate more on local objectives led to the inclusion of the technical assistant consultants and determined the detailed information that is collected in OTIS.

Because a large proportion of local health departments were working on similar objectives, such as increasing compliance with the state's smoke-free workplace law (60 percent) and decreasing tobacco sales to minors (61 percent), we now are in a position to examine data in a systematic way to determine the probable reasons for success. Given that the "Local Program Evaluation Planning Guide" (Tang, Koumjian, Cowling, and Roeseler, 2001) suggests specific data collection instruments and protocols, the data are expected to be reasonably comparable. Even though methodologies and quality may differ, we will be able to statistically examine the most methodologically similar, high-quality evaluations. In addition, profiles can be created that contain information on the strength of tobacco control for each local health department, similar to the concept described by Stillman and others (1999). Also we will include a variable in the model to measure the level of Communities of Excellence acceptance by the local health department, incorporating both objective and subjective data. The analysis will help us determine the relative strength of certain strategies for an intervention in comparison to the strength of tobacco control for that local health department. Programmatically, this should help state TCP staff to strategically market specific interventions to the local health departments and to work on improving the skills of local health departments to increase the strength of their tobacco control programs.

Conclusion

The concepts of empowerment evaluation that were implemented by the California TCP for local program evaluation have enabled the state program to scientifically fulfill the ambitious statutory mandate to evaluate California's statewide TCP. Over the course of three evolutionary stages of local program evaluation experience, lessons have been learned that have strengthened and improved the quality of evaluation.

First, a centralized effort to evaluate local tobacco control efforts was unable to adequately capture or attribute change to local program efforts. The sheer number of local projects, combined with the diversity in their scope and focus, did not lend itself to nonspecific assessment tools that were not sensitive to local program emphases. TCP has decentralized its local program evaluation. Decentralization provides the ability to tailor evaluation to local program emphases while using uniform measures wherever possible and appropriate. It also provides the ability to group and analyze the evaluation findings of "like" interventions that address a specific tobacco control indicator. In this way, TCP will be able to gain a better understanding of what works, for whom, and under what conditions.

Second, high-quality local program evaluation does not result from the simple act of issuing recommendations for evaluation. It is the result of making evaluation a mandatory requirement for funding, persistently tracking the implementation of the requirements, and providing tailored technical assistance by highly knowledgeable people. This requires a significant commitment of time and human resources by the funding agency.

Third, local health departments and community-based organizations do not universally value evaluation. TCP's requirements for evaluation generated feelings of fear, defensiveness, and animosity.

Fourth, technical assistance is most valuable when it is specifically tailored to the interventions being carried out by funded agencies. In the early years of the California TCP, general training sessions were conducted that focused on the fundamentals of evaluation design and sampling. In hindsight, it is evident that local projects had difficulty applying general information to their specific circumstances. TCP now provides detailed sample evaluation designs for typical objectives appropriate for local programs, and it makes expert individual technical assistance available.

Fifth, program staff and local program evaluators frequently speak in different languages, hold different values, and have different expectations, which they either do not or cannot successfully share with one another. Facilitating better communication and understanding between program staff and local program evaluators has been an important component of TCP's efforts to improve local program evaluation. TCP provides tip sheets on how to select an evaluator, provides joint trainings and technical assistance opportunities for program staff and local program evaluators, and has convened a workgroup made up of program staff and evaluators to develop technical assistance tools and training activities that mutually meet the needs of program staff and evaluators.

And finally, although the community and state colleges provide rich human resources steeped in program evaluation expertise, many evaluators are not experienced at evaluating community-level change. They are frequently more knowledgeable and comfortable designing and conducting evaluations that measure individual changes in knowledge, attitudes, beliefs, and behaviors. TCP uses its procurements, technical assistance documents, and trainings and conferences to explain, provide examples, and model evaluation designs that focus on community-level change.

Interestingly, the California TCP began moving toward an empowerment evaluation model during the second stage of its local program evaluation, but this happened in response to the needs of local programs and not because of any formal theoretical framework having been adopted. The experience of a large-scale state program such as the California TCP made apparent the serious limitations of a more traditional evaluation approaches in which an independent researcher was selected to evaluate hundreds of local programs. It is simply not practical for an independent contractor to evaluate two hundred diverse local programs. An empowerment evaluation, with its emphasis on self-assessment, facilitation, and capacity building can meet the challenges of this diversity yet guarantee that the evaluation will strengthen the individual local programs.

Although the Communities of Excellence assessment model and the OTIS reporting system have only been applied to local health departments, TCP plans to expand their application to its more than one hundred competitive grantees. These include community-based, regional, and statewide projects operated by community organizations, coalitions, and university-based research institutions.

Although TCP currently applies the concepts of empowerment evaluation to local program evaluation, it diverges from the standard approach in certain important respects. For example, unlike many other programs that have used empowerment evaluation, TCP requires that local evaluators, whether program staff members or contractors, meet certain minimum qualifications. They must meet specified educational and work experience criteria. These requirements enable them to be empowered more easily to face the dynamic tobacco control movement in California. Another modification is that TCP allows local program evaluators to be either local program staff or external consultants. Early on, however, it became apparent that many local programs contracted with local program evaluators who did not have expertise in conducting evaluations that focused on policy development and social norm change. The establishment of the technical assistant consultant system provided an extra level of technical support for local program evaluators and is helping to remedy this situation. The local program evaluators also work closely with TCP's local program staff. As a result, the local program evaluators have improved their skills and have established strong relationships with local programs. Some of the differences between TCP's evaluation and "classic" empowerment evaluation come from TCP applying the concepts of empowerment evaluation *after* a system for local program evaluation was created and evolved. However, most of the differences are necessary to meet the unique situations of TCP or of the local programs.

The use of results from local program evaluations, incorporated with surveillance data and other special projects, has enormous potential to accomplish a comprehensive evaluation for the state program. After the second stage, TCP was able to aggregate outcome evaluation data from some local programs to assess the change and impact on specific tobacco control areas, such as smoke-free bar compliance, voluntary smoke-free-home policy adoption, and the illegal sale of tobacco to minors. Inferential analysis can show the relationship between tobacco use outcomes such as smoking prevalence or secondhand smoke exposure and local program activities. Meanwhile, the review of the individual local program evaluation results can help a state agency to identify best practices for future promotion.

Because the state agency is accountable for the use of public funds, a high-quality and credible comprehensive evaluation for the state program is indispensable. This case study on how to evaluate the performance of local programs and their contribution to a comprehensive statewide program evaluation demonstrates one approach to managing evaluation challenges posed by multiple community-based or local programs and components of a large statewide, government-funded program.

References

Albright, A., Howard-Pitney, B., Roberts, S., and Zicarelli, J. *Tell Your Story: Guidelines for Preparing and Evaluation Report.* Sacramento: California Department of Health Services, 1998.

California Department of Health Services. *Compendium of Abstracts-Evaluation Showcase: Project Director's Meeting 1999.* Sacramento: California Department of Health Services, 1999.

California Health and Safety Code §104375. *West's Annotated California Codes: Health and Safety Code Sections 102100 to 115699.* St. Paul, Minn.: West, 1996.

Edith, D. B. *Using Case Studies to Do Program Evaluation.* Sacramento: California Department of Health Services, 1999.

Fetterman, D. M. "Empowerment Evaluation." *Evaluation Practice,* 1994a, *15,* 1–15.

Fetterman, D. M. "Steps of Empowerment Evaluation: From California to Cape Town." *Evaluation and Program Planning,* 1994b, *17,* 305–313.

Fetterman, D. M. "Empowerment Evaluation: An Introduction to Theory and Practice." In D. M. Fetterman, S. J. Kaftarian, and A. Wandersman (eds.), *Empowerment Evaluation: Knowledge and Tools for Self-assessment and Accountability.* Thousand Oaks, Calif.: Sage, 1996.

Malarcher, A. M., Schulman, J., Epstein, L. A., Thun, M. J., Mowery, P., Pierce, B., Escobedo, L., and Giovino, G. "Methodological Issues in Estimating Smoking-Attributable Mortality in the United States." *American Journal of Epidemiology,* 2000, *152,* 573–584.

Rossi, P. H., Freeman, H. E., and Lipsey, M. W. *Evaluation: A Systematic Approach.* Thousand Oaks, Calif.: Sage, 1999.

Shadish, W. R., Cook, T. D., and Leviton, L. C. *Foundations of Program Evaluation: Theories of Practice.* Thousand Oaks, Calif.: Sage, 1991.

Stillman, F., Hartman, A., Graubard, B., Gilpin, E., Chavis, D., Garcia, J., Wun, L. M., Lynn, L., and Manley, M. "The American Stop Smoking Intervention Study: Conceptual Framework and Evaluation Design." *Evaluation Review,* 1999, *23,* 259–280.

Tang, H., Koumjian, K., Cowling, D., and Roeseler, A. *Local Program Evaluation Planning Guide*. Sacramento: California Department of Health Services, 2001.

The Gallup Organization. *Independent Evaluation (IE) of the California Tobacco Control Prevention and Education Program: Waves 1,2, and 3*. Rockville, Md.: The Gallup Organization, 2000.

Zimmerman, M. A. "Empowerment Theory: Psychological, Organizational, and Community Levels of Analysis." In J. Rappaport and E. Seidman (eds.), *Handbook of Community Psychology*. New York: Plenum Press, 2000.

HAO TANG *is a research scientist for the California Department of Health Services Tobacco Control Section.*

DAVID W. COWLING *is a research scientist for the California Department of Health Services Tobacco Control Section.*

KRISTI KOUMJIAN *is a research scientist for the California Department of Health Services Tobacco Control Section.*

APRIL ROESELER *is the chief of the California Department of Health Services Tobacco Control Section, Local Programs and Evaluation.*

JON LLOYD *is the chief of the California Department of Health Services Tobacco Control Section, Data Analysis and Evaluation Unit.*

TODD ROGERS *is a senior evaluation consultant to California Department of Health Services Tobacco Control Section.*

4

Evaluators must operate in a multicontextual environment with multiple stakeholders. As the hierarchy of stakeholders becomes more complex, evaluators must react to and work within the ecological environment in which their evaluated programs are conducted. Recognizing the factors that influence the evaluation plan and knowing the best strategies in dealing with different authorizing environments can reduce the difficulty of negotiating with multiple stakeholders and increase the evaluation's validity.

Community-Based Organizations and State Initiatives: The Negotiation Process of Program Evaluation

Bianca L. Guzmán, Aida Feria

States have become powerful authorizing environments for creating policies focused on the evaluation of social welfare programs (Bell, 1994; Patton, 1997; Posavac and Carey, 1997). State-mandated evaluation policies create an environment wherein community-based organizations that receive grant contracts must constantly negotiate evaluation plans, not only with the state but with other critical stakeholders. The renegotiation process between key stakeholders can present many challenges for the completion of an effective evaluation plan. This chapter outlines the major challenges associated with conducting program evaluation in today's system of multilevel stakeholders. It concludes by offering recommendations derived from the experiences of conducting a program evaluation in which several stakeholders were intrinsically involved in the evaluation process and results.

Community-Based Organizations

Community-based organizations (CBOs) are in a unique position to carry forth programming of intervention or prevention programs and also assume responsibility for evaluation activities (Patton, 1997). Many CBOs

This work was funded in part by the Department of Health Services, Community Challenge Grants, and Grant no. 99–85636. We want to thank Michele Schlehofer-Sutton, Ryan Whetstone, and Juan R. Urdiales for their valuable assistance in the formatting of this manuscript. Finally, we want to thank all the individuals who work at CHOICES for their dedication to the issues of adolescent sexual health.

have community connections that can be vital to program implementation. Unlike large state agencies, well-established CBOs have the ability to enlist the support of local stakeholders for the process of evaluation. In the case of our organization, CHOICES (The CHOICES Organization), we have established community support with many key community stakeholders such as school officials, local political leaders, public health organizations, and the clergy. CHOICES is a small organization that has operated in the community for twelve years, focusing primarily on intervention programming to prevent teenage pregnancy and encourage reproductive health care for multi-ethnic urban youth and their families. A small evaluation unit conducts several levels of evaluation with most of the programs that are administered. It is important to note that the CHOICES evaluation unit tends to be highly involved in creating interventions and in grant-writing activities. We believe that having the evaluation team participate in programming creates evaluation plans that are highly congruent with both the short- and long-term goals of the interventions we conduct.

When CHOICES was awarded a grant by the Community Challenge Grant (CCG) program in 1996, we had much to learn regarding the political environment in which evaluations take place. The following section details the challenges faced in conducting a program evaluation with multiple stakeholders.

A State Initiative

California created the CCG program in 1996 in response to the high number of teenage pregnancies in the state (California Department of Health Services, 2002). This $20-million program has been administered through the State Department of Health (Welfare and Institutions Code, Sec. 19883–18993.9). Since the inception of the program, the state has created a competitive grants process for allocating funds to eligible parties. As part of the grant submission and award process, organizations have been required to submit an evaluation plan and participate in the statewide and local evaluation processes.

The request for applications indicated that programs must participate in both process and outcome evaluations. The statewide evaluation requirements stipulated that an independent contractor would be responsible for creating the protocol for all evaluation activities of the funded programs. Funded programs were responsible for creating a local evaluation to demonstrate effectiveness for their particular program as well. According to the request for applications, *process evaluation* was defined as a review of documentation that the proposed project activities or interventions were carried out as planned. The outcome evaluation required evidence of whether or not the documented intervention resulted in the attainment of short-term program goals (State of California Department of Health Services, 1996). Grants were awarded to approximately 113 local projects in CBOs, school districts, and public health and social service agencies.

Negotiations with State Stakeholders

When we were first awarded the grant, we had definitive plans for the evaluation process. Once we signed the contract with the state, we believed that we could begin programming and evaluation activities immediately. One of the first lessons we learned was that a competitive grant process that stipulates that an independent contractor conduct the statewide evaluation component can be taxing on individual CBOs. We learned that the state first had to secure a contract with one organization, such as an evaluation firm or educational institution, to develop a methodology for evaluating all funded programs. From the onset of the grant process, there had not been an independent contractor assigned to create a state-level protocol for evaluation. This meant that we could not begin programming or evaluation activities until we understood the still-developing evaluation guidelines of the state evaluation team. In this instance, as an evaluation unit of a CBO, we felt extremely powerless because we were unable to conduct evaluation until one or more protocols had been developed and released by the state.

Once the state had secured an independent contractor, we learned that there would be a single evaluation tool that all 113 agencies would use to assess statewide evaluation impact. The CHOICES executive director and director of evaluation, along with other executive directors and evaluators from the agencies receiving these grants, felt that use of a single evaluation tool was not the most appropriate way to assess program impact. All were concerned with the sensitivity and validity of using one tool when programs were being conducted by so many different types of organizations. Nevertheless, we were required to participate in the statewide evaluation.

This situation presented an opportunity for interactions between the state and us, as well as with staff from other awarded agencies. Staff from several of these agencies, including ours, attempted to renegotiate evaluation plans. We asked the state to view more critically the lack of sensitivity of a single protocol to diverse outcomes and the inferences that might be drawn from the approved state evaluation protocol. We also understood that each participating agency would need the assistance of the state evaluators to justify changes to the protocol. For inexperienced or even experienced evaluators, conflicts at this level among stakeholders can be unnerving. Nevertheless, we suggest that these conflicts are rather common occurrences when dealing with large bureaucratic organizations such as the State of California.

The negotiation process with the state was a long one. Even so, given our status as a fairly experienced CBO, we had already learned to approach large authorizing environments such as the state with neutrality and calm. The main approach of all the stakeholders involved, including the executive directors and the evaluators, was to suggest to the state that the evaluation protocol could include multiple versions of a survey to assess program impact. The selection of a version could be determined within the context of specific program activities and target audiences. For example, if an agency were conducting parenting courses for pregnant teenagers, the evaluation protocol might ask questions regarding what the participants learned in the parenting course. Alternatively, if an agency were conducting a teenage pregnancy prevention program, the evaluation protocol might ask questions regarding how many teens reported condom use.

The stakeholders and evaluators were able to successfully negotiate with the state over the course of nearly a year, such that the state agreed to reformat the evaluation tool to include multilevel goals for different types of programming. In the meantime, CBOs had begun their programming without any state-approved evaluation protocols in place. Thus the state had lost an opportunity to evaluate projects from the onset of programming. For the individual stakeholder agencies, the delay cost them the ability to confidently attribute observed changes to their programs because they were limited to using the state evaluation tool. Moreover, neither stakeholders nor evaluators may be completely satisfied with the result of the negotiations relative to stakeholder interests. However, all were agreed that the resulting approach was stronger than the initial one. It should be noted that, as of early 2002, there was a new request for applications for this initiative that detailed a new set of criteria for state and local evaluations (for additional information, visit www.dhs.ca.gov).

In the following sections, we turn our attention to how we conducted and negotiated evaluation at the local level.

Ecological Context as an Influence on Stakeholders

One of the first challenges CHOICES faced when addressing community stakeholders was the issue of "selling" the program. Among the goals of CHOICES was to obtain approval from the community to conduct a teenage pregnancy prevention and intervention program and to evaluate this effort. However, community approval could not be obtained until concerns of key community stakeholders were properly addressed. We felt it was necessary for the evaluation team to be involved, along with the executive director in this negotiation process, because the expertise of the evaluators would add credibility to the proposed program.

Teenage pregnancy, like many other socially charged issues, is a topic that's political in nature (Jemmott, Jemmott, Fong, and McCaffree, 1999). Community members, local political leaders, and the clergy usually have firm opinions about what constitutes socially deviant behavior (Francoeur, 1990; Garnier, Stein, and Jacobs, 1997; Nash and Bowen, 1999). There is clear evidence and direction in the legal arena about what should be done with teenagers who use drugs and alcohol, as well as those who engage in many other forms of social deviance such as violence (Simone and others, 2000). We have found that with teenage pregnancy, communities often find it difficult to have a clear direction about what should be done. This lack of direction might be partly due to the idea that teenage pregnancy is the outcome of sexual behavior of adolescents who usually are not married. Sexuality among teens in communities where there are strict norms about not having sex before marriage, such as the community in which we were working, carries negative moral judgment but no specific details about how the community ought to behave (Francoeur, 1990). That is, members of a community may have a hard time deciding whether their community ought to become involved in programming for individuals who are not morally worthy of social programming (Gomez and Van Oss Marin, 1996). These issues are important for evaluators to consider, because many evaluators find themselves evaluating programs that are socially controversial. We mention these issues because they are highly relevant to defining the environment for programming and evaluation.

Larger Metaculture. Social structure has serious implications for whether and how stakeholders will allow the process of evaluation to flourish (Levine and Perkins, 1997). As Bronfenbrenner's ecological model (1979) suggests, human behavior is embedded in a hierarchy of metaculture. This hierarchy ranges from the *macrosystem* level (for example, national norms and values), through *exosystem*-level forces (for example, state norms), down to *mesosystem*-level forces (for example, community norms), and finally to *microsystem*-level forces (for example, guiding principles of a CBO). Therefore, evaluators must clearly define the metaculture of each of the key stakeholders. In the case of our evaluation, the larger U.S. culture was the macrosystem in which teenage pregnancy was defined. The exosystem included the State of California, along with other state-level norms. The mesosystem included individual community norms, and the microsystem involved the values of CHOICES (see Figure 4.1). The process of defining metaculture can only be conducted once the evaluator has identified the hierarchy of key stakeholders of a particular community that will be involved in the evaluation process.

Identifying the Hierarchy of Key Stakeholders. As we mentioned previously, the State of California was one of the key stakeholders with which the evaluation team and the executive director had to initially negotiate the details of the programming and evaluation. The state was clear that one of the performance outcomes of a program should be the reduction of teenage pregnancy. The state insisted that there had to be a systematic impact evaluation of the program in order to claim program success. The state did not stipulate how and where the program should be implemented or with what population.

From the standpoint of CHOICES, we felt that school settings were and continue to be one of the most appropriate places to educate youth about many social issues. Indeed, sex education programs are becoming increasingly present in many public schools (Finkel and Finkel, 1985). Youth in the United States spend a significant amount of their time in a school setting; therefore, school settings are socializing agents for youth and ideal places in which to carry out social service programming (Kirby, 1985,

Figure 4.1. The Ecological Context of CHOICES

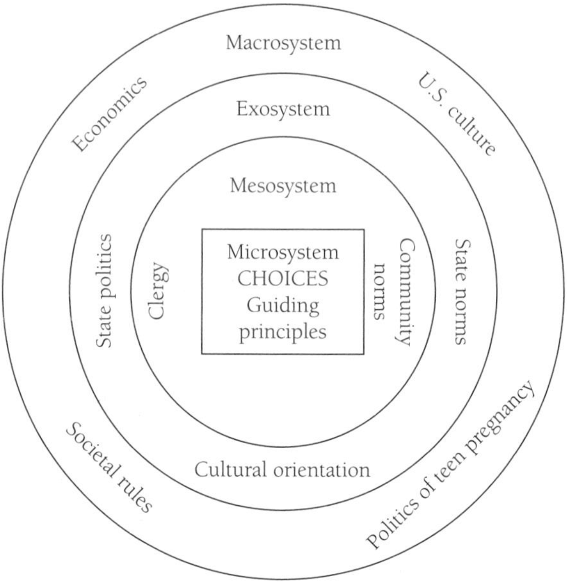

2000). Two other reasons that many CBOs target public schools as a place to conduct social service programs are that (1) youth enrolled in public schools are the most accurate representation of a healthy adolescent population, and (2) youth who attend public schools are easily accessible. Therefore, CHOICES and its evaluation team had to identify the ecological environment of the next stakeholder to be involved in our evaluation, which was the local school district.

Hierarchy in Local School Districts

Establishing evaluation plans in a public school district with school-aged youth can present evaluators with many implementation issues (Felner, 2000). One of the first issues to consider is who holds the power to make decisions regarding how evaluations will take place. When we examined the hierarchy of local school districts, we quickly learned that the most powerful decision makers are the board members and the superintendent of the district. The next tier in authority is made up of the school principals, followed by assistant principals, counselors, and classroom teachers. Parents are a key stakeholder group and have what might be called indirect authority; they can choose to block participation of their children in the evaluation. Although students may be key stakeholders, they have little authority in a school-based setting to influence whether or not evaluation activities occur. As to the subject of the evaluation, students can influence the accuracy and

Figure 4.2. Hierarchy of Authorities and Factors That Influence Evaluation Implementation

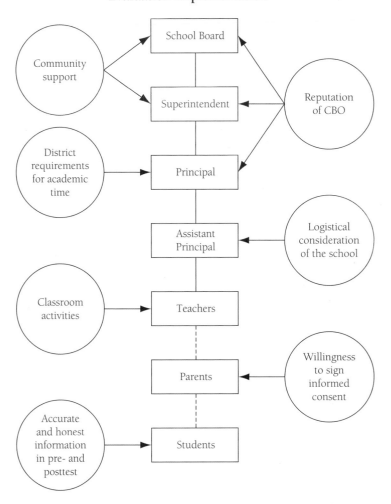

reliability of evaluation results, because they ultimately control the extent to which the information they provide is truthful and candid.

It is important to understand the chain of command before negotiating with stakeholders who have the authority and ability to make decisions at different points in the evaluation process (see Figure 4.2). We understand that the metaculture of key stakeholders may include stakeholders who have different levels of authority and that these stakeholders constantly interact with each other in large organizations such as school districts. The sections that follow isolate the different levels of authority in a school district to discuss and illustrate several points. However, readers must be cautioned that there are few instances in which these stakeholders work in isolation from each other.

School Board Members and Superintendent. School board members are the stakeholder group that has the most influence over the superintendent of a school district. These stakeholders are the gatekeepers for allowing evaluation plans to be approved at the policy level. As one assistant principal said to us, "If the school board decides [votes] yes, then it happens." If school board members direct that a certain program be implemented, the superintendent generally must implement the program. Therefore, evaluators must be prepared to attend school board meetings along with the executive director to propose programming and the accompanying evaluation activities. The evaluators must also allow these stakeholders to have some input into the evaluation plans, which could potentially lead to changes in those plans. As a final caveat, this process needs to be accomplished in a way that allows the evaluator to maintain sufficient control over the evaluation to reasonably determine program impact in addition to, or perhaps in spite of, changes that might be requested in the plans by key stakeholders.

Obtaining approval from a school board requires local political leaders to support the CBO, which is conducting the evaluation. In our case, we found it extremely useful to have city council members write letters of support for the program to the school board. It is also important to have local political leaders, such as the mayor of the city, attend school board meetings and give verbal approval of the program once it has been presented to the board. There will always be school board members who are not supportive of the program. Thus the goal of the evaluator should be to obtain approval from the most powerful or influential leaders of the board. If this is not possible, the next step ought to be to obtain approval from a majority of the board members and have the support of the superintendent.

Principals and Assistant Principals. Once approval is obtained from the highest authorities (the board and the superintendent), it would seem that evaluators would be free to conduct their evaluations. Unfortunately, this is not always the case. The negotiation process continues at the local school level. Once evaluators reach this level, the most powerful stakeholder is the principal, generally followed by the assistant principal. In some schools, the principal delegates to the assistant principal those duties involved with negotiating with outside agencies. Whenever possible, it is important to have the support of both the principal and assistant principal. By the time evaluators schedule an appointment with the principal, it is likely that she or he has already had some sort of correspondence with the superintendent about the program you are proposing. As an evaluator, you may not be aware of how or whether this contact was made. The superintendent may have issued a standard memo stating that the district has allowed a teenage pregnancy prevention program to be implemented in the school district. This information may have come to the principals at a meeting or through telephone conversations with the superintendent. The point here is that the evaluator may not be fully aware of the social context in which the superintendent granted permission for the evaluation to go forward. However, the social context of the authorizing environment sets the stage for how the principals will interact with the evaluation team.

We were reminded of this when we dealt with two different school districts regarding CHOICES. One superintendent personally contacted all of the principals who were to be involved in the evaluation. This superintendent was highly supportive of our project and made the calls to the principals while the executive director and evaluation staff were present in his office. He established a positive tone for the evaluation activities by stating that the board had just approved this "great project" to prevent teenage pregnancy in the district. He mentioned that he really wanted the principals and their staff to assist CHOICES in any way possible. This experience stands in marked contrast to our experience with another superintendent who was not highly supportive of our program. He sent out letters to each individual school principal stating that our project had been approved but did not suggest that the school assist in either the programming or evaluation efforts. The tone of the first message set the stage for a positive interaction, whereas the neutral, if not detached, tone of the second message may have left the principals unsure as to how to interact with or what to expect from the CBO evaluation team.

A key issue to consider at this stage is that, although a program may have school board approval, the negotiation process is not complete. In our experience, some principals are extremely receptive but others are not. We worked with a total of nine schools in which every principal had different priorities, goals, and parameters within which programs were to be implemented and evaluated.

One of the key issues related to evaluation in a school setting is whether the evaluation will take place during academic school time or in an after-school setting (Kirby, 2000). In our twelve years of experience, we have found that when we conduct programming or evaluation activities in an after-school setting, the rate of participation is much reduced, regardless of what type of programming is being delivered. This has been the case, whether or not there was compensation involved for the participants. In either case, there are significant implications for determining the level and impact of program success.

The timing of the program and evaluation activities is a key issue that evaluators must determine early in the evaluation planning process. Schools tend to be more receptive to allowing programming if it is on an after-school basis. It is much more difficult to negotiate to conduct programming during academic school time. The priority of school principals is to ensure that their students receive adequate academic instruction. We found that many principals may feel that if a large portion of the school day is devoted to outside programming, students are distracted from academic learning. Therefore, the negotiation of time is one of the first obstacles that an evaluator will face. Clearly, our suggestion is to negotiate for programming and evaluation during academic time while students are engaged in a school setting. The reality of negotiation for some evaluators, however, may mean that programming and evaluation are done after school. In this case, evaluators must plan around the issue of attrition of participants.

In the case of CHOICES, we wanted to conduct approximately four hours of programming and evaluation during academic time. The intervention involved a theater performance followed by a debriefing workshop. The basic evaluation plan was to administer pre- and posttests to participants who attended the theater performance (for a more detailed description of the evaluation, see Guzmán and Feria, 2001; Guzmán and others, 2001; and Guzmán and others, 2002; drafts available from the first author on request). Our goal was to negotiate with the school principals for at least five hours of academic time. Several principals expressed concern about this, citing the time already being taken from teaching and learning for required testing. Concerns about time taken away from instruction must be considered, no matter how beneficial a program might be. Outside of testing, schools have athletic and social events at different points during the year in which the whole student body will be involved; football season is an example. Therefore, evaluators must be aware of the academic and extracurricular calendars for each school and be able to allow for flexibility in their programming if they wish to be able to negotiate successfully with a school principal.

Teachers. Once the principal and assistant principals have been enlisted in the evaluation process, the final level of authority is the classroom teachers. Teachers are the key to collecting relevant evaluation data. In some schools, evaluators will find that teachers are highly vested in the issue proposed by the programming and evaluation activities. In contrast, some teachers say that adding outside programming activities is an additional burden beyond their already extensive classroom responsibilities. With our program, teachers assisted us by distributing and collecting the consent forms that parents needed to fill out before students could participate in the evaluation process. State guidelines require that evaluations conducted during academic school time where a student is involved in an evaluation must have active informed consent from their parent or legal guardian to participate. "Active consent" means that every participant must have a signed parental consent form on file before they can participate in the evaluation (Ross, Sundberg, and Flint, 1999). Therefore, enlisting the support of the teachers is imperative to being able to conduct our evaluation. In addition to being critical stakeholders during this process, teachers can either facilitate or complicate other evaluation components.

In our evaluation process, we found that, although teachers were required to participate, some were unwilling to give us full cooperation. For example, a principal may have agreed to our being in a classroom for a whole period. However, once we got to the classroom, the teacher would say that the students were taking a test that day so we had only thirty minutes, thus putting everybody in a difficult situation. There are several choices to be made, however, and as an evaluator, one must be careful; those choices can affect the overall agreement of the school with regard to the programming being conducted. In our case, we attempted to negotiate with the teacher first if at all possible. If the teacher was unwilling to negotiate, and it was critical that we have the time, we asked if we could come back another day. This of course had implications for the evaluation plan. The reality of the situation means that an evaluator either negotiates a new strategy or makes a decision about whether the programming ought to continue in that school. Thorough evaluation planning can account for many of these contingencies so that the evaluator's response to such situations is consistent and that inconsistent implementation does not pose a threat to the validity of the evaluation findings.

Lessons to Keep in Mind. We have discussed the hierarchy of a typical school district and how the different stakeholders might be approached. Some evaluators may be tempted to approach a district in a different manner in order to save time. However, a different approach might put a credible CBO with a competent evaluation team in jeopardy if school district protocols are not followed. For example, we have seen instances in which an evaluator contacts a classroom teacher or a counselor about the implementation of an evaluation program. Although technically a teacher has authority over the classroom, he or she cannot legally make decisions about program implementation and evaluation without informing the principal, who is then responsible for deciding whether the superintendent must also be contacted. With topics such as teenage pregnancy, it has been our experience that few teachers can risk their careers and allow programming in their classroom without the clearance of the principal. By the same token, once the principal is briefed, she or he is unlikely to grant permission unless the superintendent is well aware of the program and has approved it in writing. As has been stated previously, teenage pregnancy is a socially and morally charged issue, so there are many reasons why it is critically important to follow the chain of command when establishing evaluation plans. This is also the case for many other socially charged issues such as drug and violence prevention.

In our case, it was very difficult to enlist the support of the school districts, and it would have been a grave mistake for us to contact an individual teacher as a starting point in our negotiation process. That is to say, if we had allowed a teacher to negotiate for us with the principal and superintendent, we would have almost certainly been denied entrance into the school district. The teacher would not have had sufficient knowledge and authority to speak on our behalf. Over years of experience in conducting evaluations, we have found many supportive teachers who are well intentioned and want to see the issue of teenage pregnancy addressed in their school. Although having supportive teachers is very important, it does not guarantee that the school administrators will have the same reactions to social service programs being conducted during academic time. The lesson learned is that there is no short-cut regarding a thorough understanding of the needs of various stakeholders in the authorizing environment and that a thorough and competent evaluation plan will take this into account.

Fluidity of Negotiation

Although an evaluation plan may have been negotiated with all the stake-holders, it is safe to say that the negotiation process is never final. That is, even when a district has given approval, it is a temporary agreement at best. In our experience, we have found that new school board members, replacement principals, and new teachers may have opinions that differ from the individuals with whom the evaluation plan was originally negotiated. We also found that we were in a constant negotiation process with stakehold-ers at one or more of the nine schools in which we conducted program eval-uations. Program evaluators must be prepared to include this facet of evaluation in their evaluation timeline. We have found this portion of the evaluation process to be the most challenging aspect of completing an eval-uation, especially when there are new stakeholders coming on board mid-way during an evaluation. Therefore, evaluators must always be prepared to amend their evaluation plans at any stage of the evaluation process or risk being unable to conduct any evaluation activities.

Issue of Acceptability

Although traditional approaches to evaluation methodology might posit that ongoing changes in the evaluation plan decrease the plan's usefulness and potentially its internal validity, it is important to note that changing the evaluation plan continuously does not inherently mean that evalua-tion results are less valid. In actuality, we propose that changing the eval-uation plan to meet the specific needs of the program and of those parties involved in its implementation, including participants, might actually *increase* the acceptability and usefulness of the evaluation findings with-out necessarily affecting the validity of the evaluation.

Although this notion may seem contradictory to traditional method-ological approaches, it is in line with the ecological model proposed by Bronfenbrenner (1979). Considering that programs and their accompany-ing evaluation plans are conducted in community settings, these programs are inherently implemented and evaluated in a constantly changing ecolog-ical environment (Levine and Perkins, 1997). This means that the needs of stakeholders, the broader community, and the target populations are con-stantly being shaped and adjusted by contextual factors at the macrosystem, exosystem, mesosystem, and microsystem levels. Indeed, when viewed in its ecological context, the specific needs of the target population *should* change throughout the course of program implementation and evaluation; it may even be the case that the initial problem or concern prompting the need for the program has changed or resolved itself. As a result, evaluation plans should adapt themselves over time to meet these changing needs (Posavac and Carey, 1997).

We do not intend to encourage evaluators to implement inconsistent evaluation activities that can potentially lead to participant selection bias. And we are not suggesting that evaluators negotiate with only certain types of schools that have administrators who are willing to participate in evaluation activities. Instead, what we are emphasizing is that evaluators must be aware of how social contexts may change and must prepare their evaluation plans to include negotiation activities with all stakeholders involved. In our case, we have continuously modified our evaluation plans and have been able to demonstrate program impact on a yearly basis for the last six years (see Guzmán and Feria, 2001; Guzmán and others, 2001, for more details).

Recommendations and Conclusions

Clearly, negotiating and conducting an evaluation plan in a community-based setting is not an easy task. Dealing with multiple key stakeholders can present program evaluators with new challenges, as this necessitates the need to negotiate with individuals who have a variety of interests and motives regarding the program and its evaluation. We therefore offer the following recommendations to assist evaluators with this process:

• *Identify who the key stakeholders are.* What is the hierarchy? What are the needs of the stakeholders? As evaluators working with multiple stakeholders in a multilevel system, it is essential to know the needs of all key stakeholders involved and how stakeholders' needs may differ. Ideally, the evaluation plan should meet the needs of every key stakeholder. It is in the best interest of an evaluator to guide stakeholders through the process of negotiation to come to these agreements. This may take some negotiating skills and creativity on the part of the evaluator. However, evaluators should realize that the needs of every key stakeholder are rarely met in their entirety; consequently, the goal of the evaluator is to meet stakeholders' needs sufficiently well to implement a meaningful program and conduct evaluation activities capable of indicating program efficacy. Moreover, evaluators must remember that the evaluation plan should have sufficient objectivity to meet the goals to be accomplished by a particular program. The evaluator must also realize that some independence and autonomy may be lost in negotiating with key stakeholders. However, the integrity of the programming and evaluation, as well as the guiding principles of a particular CBO or evaluator, should not be compromised.

• *Research the environment in which the program will be implemented.* This is a crucial component in understanding the needs of key stakeholders. It includes not only recognizing the direct influences on stakeholders, such as state mandates and available funding and time allotted to program implementation and evaluation, but the indirect influences of stakeholders, such as social and cultural norms, community leaders, business owners, and the needs of participants and their families.

• *Negotiate through the hierarchy.* One important thing to do when negotiating the evaluation plan is to start your negotiations with the most influential stakeholders and get them to support your evaluation plan. After that, proceed down the hierarchy of stakeholders until an overall agreement is reached. Proceeding in this manner generally makes the negotiation process run more smoothly and may help avoid legal complications that could arise if someone unauthorized is called upon to make decisions affecting the evaluation plan.

• *Seek out the support of people who indirectly influence the stakeholder.* Key individuals in the community, such as business owners, clergy members, youth group organizations, local political leaders, and individuals in the media, may have the ability to indirectly influence stakeholders to view the program and evaluation plan favorably. Thus it may be in the best interest of all parties involved if the support of these individuals is sought while also obtaining support for your program directly from key stakeholders.

• *Be willing to renegotiate the plan on an ongoing basis.* Because key stakeholders' needs may change or key stakeholders themselves may change, it is necessary to be willing to rework the evaluation plan to meet the evolving needs of these individuals. The process of re-evaluating the plan to meet the changing needs of key stakeholders will not only work to maintain interest in and support for your evaluation plan but may also increase the sensitivity of the design and, in turn, increase support for your evaluation findings.

In conclusion, implementing an evaluation plan in a community-based setting with multiple layers of stakeholders requiring negotiation and agreement may be an overwhelming task for even the most seasoned evaluators. Nevertheless, multicontextual environments are becoming increasingly commonplace in today's society. By recognizing that multicontextual considerations can strengthen the evaluation plan and by knowing the best tactics to use when dealing with different authorizing environments, evaluators can both significantly mitigate the difficulty of dealing with multiple stakeholders and increase the usefulness of their evaluation findings.

References

Bell, J. B. "Managing Evaluation Projects Step by Step." In J. S. Wholey, H. P. Hatry, and K. E. Newcomer (eds.), *Handbook of Practical Program Evaluation*. San Francisco: Jossey-Bass, 1994.

Bronfenbrenner, U. *The Ecology of Human Development Experiments by Nature and Design.* Cambridge, Mass.: Harvard University Press, 1979.

California Department of Health Services. *Community Challenge Grant Program: Funding Local Solutions to Reduce Teen and Unwed Pregnancies and Fatherlessness.* Sacramento, Calif.: Office of Community Challenge Grants, Oct. 1996.

California Department of Health Services. *Making the Connection between Youth Development and Teen Pregnancy Prevention Programs Request for Application.* Sacramento, Calif.: Office of Family Planning, Jan. 2002.

Felner, R. D. "Educational Reform as Ecologically-Based Prevention and Promotion: The Project on High Performance Learning Communities." In D. Cicchetti, J. Rappaport, I. Sandler, and R. Weissberg (eds.), *The Promotion of Wellness in Children and Adolescents.* Washington, D.C.: Child Welfare League of America, 2000.

Finkel, M. L., and Finkel, S. "Sex Education in High School." *Society,* Nov.-Dec. 1985, 48–52.

Francoeur, R. T. "Current Religious Doctrines of Sexual and Erotic Development in Childhood." In M. E. Perry (ed.), *Handbook of Sexology.* Vol. 7: *Childhood and Adolescent Sexology.* Encino, Calif.: Elsevier, 1990.

Garnier, H. E., Stein, J. A., and Jacobs, J. K. "The Process of Dropping Out of High School: A 19-Year Perspective." *American Education Research Journal,* 1997, *34,* 395–419.

Gómez, C. A., and Van Oss Marin, B. "Gender, Culture, and Power: Barriers to HIV-Prevention Strategies for Women." *Journal of Sex Research,* 1996, *33,* 355–362.

Guzmán, B. L., Casad, B. J., Schlehofer-Sutton, M. M., Feria, A., and Vasquez, E. "C.A.M.P.: A Community-based Approach to Responsible Adolescent Sexual Behavior." Manuscript under review, 2001.

Guzmán, B. L., and Feria, A. "Community Awareness Motivation Partnership (C.A.M.P.): 2001 Year End Evaluation Report." *California Department of Health Services, Community Challenge Grant Division/Responsible Parenting Initiative,* 2001.

Guzmán, B. L., Schlehofer-Sutton, M. M., Casad, B. J., Villanueva, C. M., Feria, A., and Vasquez, E. "Sex in the City: C.A.M.P. Teen Theater as a Sex Education Tool." Unpublished manuscript. Claremont Graduate University, Claremont, Calif., 2002.

Jemmott, J. B., Jemmott, L. S., Fong, G. T., and McCaffree, K. "Reducing HIV Risk-Associated Sexual Behavior Among African-American Adolescents: Testing the Generality of Intervention Effects." *American Journal of Community Psychology,* 1999, *27,* 161–187.

Kirby, D. B. "Sexuality Education: A More Realistic View of its Effects." *Journal of School Health,* 1985, *55,* 421–424.

Kirby, D. B. "School-Based Interventions to Prevent Unprotected Sex and HIV Among Adolescents." In J. Peterson and R. J. DiClemente (eds.), *Handbook of HIV Prevention.* New York: Kluwer Academic/Plenum Publishers, 2000.

Levine, M., and Perkins, D. V. *Principles of Community Psychology: Perspectives and Applications.* (2nd ed.) New York: Oxford University Press, 1997.

Nash, J. K., and Bowen, G. L. "Perceived Crime and Informal Social Control in the Neighborhood as a Context for Adolescent Behavior: A Risk and Resilience Perspective." *Social Work Research,* 1999, *23,* 171–186.

Patton, M. Q. *Utilization-Focused Evaluation: The New Century Text.* (3rd ed.) Thousand Oaks, Calif.: Sage, 1997.

Posavac, E. J., and Carey, R. G. "Chapter 1: Program Evaluation: An Overview." *Program Evaluation: Methods and Case Studies.* Englewood Cliffs, N.J: Prentice Hall, 1997.

Ross, J. G., Sundberg, E. C., and Flint, K. H. "Informed Consent in School Health Research: Why, How, and Making it Easy." *Journal of School Health,* 1999, *69,* 171–176.

Simone, A. N., Lenssen, V., Theo, A. H., Doreleijers, M., van Dijk, E., and Hartman, C. A. "Girls in Detention: What Are their Characteristics?" *Journal of Adolescence,* 2000, *23,* 2000, 287–303.

BIANCA L. GUZMÁN is director of research for The CHOICES Organization, La Puente, California.

AIDA FERIA is the director of The CHOICES Organization, La Puente, California.

5

The products and operations of program evaluation units in state legislatures have changed over the past twenty-five years. Specific changes in legislative staff's authorizing environment have had an impact on their work, including increased political competition and partisanship, term limits, and legislative access to a larger and more varied range of information. This chapter examines the current status of state legislative program evaluation.

Program Evaluation in State Legislatures: Professional Services Delivered in a Complex, Competitive Environment

Frances S. Berry, John W. Turcotte, Sarah C. Latham

To paraphrase the Oldsmobile commercial: "Today's state legislatures are not your father's institutions." Perhaps no governmental institution has changed more since the 1960s than state legislatures. This change is very evident in the post-audit function that began with a wave of post-World War II assertiveness by legislatures, expanding beyond traditional financial compliance into efficiency and program effectiveness. Legislative control of the post-audit function increased from only three states in 1951 to twenty-nine states in 1971 (Crane, 1972). The New York Legislative Commission on Expenditure Review, created in 1968, was one of the first specialized legislative program evaluation offices. In the 1970s, many state legislatures created special purpose oversight committees or directed their existing legislative post-audit organizations to conduct program evaluation or sunset reviews. By 2000, there were at least forty-four state legislative program evaluation offices; twenty-three of them had been in existence for more than twenty years; fourteen were created during the 1990s (National Conference of State Legislatures, 2001).

Program evaluation units in state legislatures today operate in an environment best characterized as more competitive, more diverse, and more influenced by partisan politics than was the case twenty-five years ago. While state legislative research operations have not been immune from national-level forces such as federal mandates, reduced fiscal assistance to the states, and policy devolution, the more salient environmental influences appear to emerge from within the states themselves. Changes directly affecting state legislatures have been widespread. Term limits for legislators, now operating in about half the states, have changed the timeframe and policy perspective of many legislators destined to leave office after six to twelve years, even if they are still popular and effective. State legislators tend to have less institutional knowledge and state-level policy experience. Legislatures are much more partisan than they used to be, and more states have competitive electoral systems (Rosenthal, 1996). Many more interest groups compete at the state level (Gray and Lowery, 1999), fracturing broad consensus building in many policy areas. A plethora of policy information is produced by think tanks representing every ideological point on the political spectrum, as well as from many other sources. The Web has brought ready information to the keyboard for citizens, legislators, and their staff. Accountability demands on the public spending process have increased as trust in government stays at a fairly low level. It should be noted, however, that traditionally in surveys of public trust, state government tends to be more positively rated than the federal government and local governments more positively rated than state governments; overall, trust in government seems to have improved in the last few years (National Academy of Public Administration, 1999).

The paradigm of legislative program evaluation has changed as well, moving away from the older paradigm of nonpartisan program evaluation staff removed from legislative influence, often in separate staff offices, producing technically proficient research under fairly independent and self-initiated conditions. The newer paradigm of legislative program evaluation is one in which staff with multidisciplinary expertise are often integrated with other legislative research units, work closely with legislators, compete with partisan staff and outside think tanks for policy relevance, and often work with less independence, under shorter timelines, producing a variety of products with more stakeholder interaction.

This chapter examines the current status of state legislative program evaluation in the twenty-first century. These offices have used new methods and information formats, integrated changing staff roles and functions, and become more proactive in meeting legislative policy information needs.

Development of Legislative Oversight and Staff Research

Alan Rosenthal (1996, p. 108) has described the decade from 1965 to 1975 as "the period of the rise of the legislative institution," when state legislatures began to transform themselves after the reapportionment lawsuits of the early 1960s. (Specifically, we refer to the U.S. Supreme Court's decisions in *Baker* v. *Carr* [1962] and *Reynolds* v. *Sims* [1964].) State legislative capacity developed during this time to take on the responsibilities that the national government had given to the states, as well as to handle more duties initiated from within state legislatures themselves. Professional staff became the backbone of improved legislative capacity, as most legislatures hired nonpartisan staff to provide research, analysis, and bill-drafting assistance to legislative committees.

Program evaluation grew out of the social science research tradition after World War II and was adopted by the federal government to evaluate the Great Society programs. In the 1970s, state legislatures also assigned professional staff to evaluate the effectiveness of programs, originally social and human service programs using the goals and methods of program evaluation. Claire Felbinger defines the evaluation of agency programs or legislative policy as "the use of scientific methods to estimate the successful implementation and resultant outcomes of programs or policies for decision making purposes" (Felbinger, 1989, p. 3). Early program evaluation focused on causality and relationships between "treatments" and results. The recession of the early 1980s and changing political philosophies led to a broader scope of program assessment encompassing both program effectiveness and operational efficiency. The 1980s and 1990s have witnessed an expansion of more varied types of evaluation, including process and implementation studies, cost-effectiveness studies, and meta-evaluations.

A common theme among writers on the development of legislative program evaluation is to note the differences and sometimes conflicts between the roles and duties of legislative auditors and program evaluation staff (for example, Chelimsky, 1994; Brooks, 1996). Traditional auditing has its intellectual home in accounting, assessing the legality and form of governmental financial transactions and management systems. During the early 1980s, an increased emphasis on productivity and efficiency within most state governments coincided with the expansion of legislative auditing to cover program performance reviews called "performance audits" and brought the auditing and program evaluation functions closer together.[1]

Legislative oversight generally and program evaluation units more specifically were shaped in the 1990s by the government accountability efforts and performance-based budgeting. Operating under recessionary pressures and a climate of "no new taxes" in the early 1990s, state legislatures turned to budget reform to hold agencies accountable for their program spending (Berry and Flowers, 1999). State budget reform proved to be a rapidly diffusing innovation with few opponents; by 1996, forty-seven out of fifty states had adopted some type of performance-based budgeting (Melkers and Willoughby, 1998). Some new program evaluation units, such as the Office of Program Policy Analysis and Government Accountability, or OPPAGA in Florida, and the Office of Performance Evaluations in Idaho, were created in conjunction with performance-based budgeting reform. In addition to conducting performance audits and policy analyses, ten of the forty-four legislative program evaluation units now assess the quality of performance measures and agency compliance with performance-based budgeting mandates; they also interpret the agency performance measurement reports to the legislatures.

Current Status of Legislative Program Evaluation

The National Legislative Program Evaluation Society (NLPES) began in 1973 and has promoted professional evaluation standards in legislative units, fifty state dialogue processes, and dissemination of best practices. In the spring of 2000, the NLPES and the National Conference of State Legislatures (NCSL) fiscal affairs committee jointly conducted a survey and study of the state legislative program evaluation offices—*Ensuring the Public Trust: How Program Policy Evaluation Serves State Legislatures* (National Conference of State Legislatures, 2001). Much of the aggregate data and information in this section comes from this study. The authors gathered other information from the following: (1) a NLPES listserv request that generated e-mail from and phone interviews of eight state legislative evaluation directors and seven senior staff, collectively from seven states (four Type 1 and three Type 2 PE units, which are described in the next section); (2) Web-site research, including state legislative program evaluation units; and (3) literature reviews.

Models of Program Evaluation Units and Operations. Although each state legislative program evaluation (PE) unit is unique in its structure and operations, we have identified two types of PE units: Type 1 and Type 2. Type 1 PE units are traditional legislative auditors or auditor generals who have expanded their financial compliance auditing to include program evaluation. These units operate independently but often report to a designated legislative committee (for example, the Arizona auditor general). Type 2 PE units are those that conduct performance audits and program evaluation that are not part of an auditor general's office. These include joint legislative committees or commissions established by law or legislative rule to provide a range of services from investigations to program evaluations and whose appointed members approve proposed findings of staff (for example, Mississippi Joint Legislative Committee on Performance Evaluation and Expenditure Review [PEER]). Type 2 also includes independent legislative offices, headed by a director, that evaluate programs and assist with fiscal oversight and performance measurement. Directors of Type 2 units perform duties independently and issue reports without committee review but under general oversight of presiding officers or by a joint audit or budget committee (for example, the Florida OPPAGA).

Table 5.1 contains the names of the forty-two nonpartisan program evaluation units identified in the NLPES study, as well as the California Office of Legislative Analyst, which has been added by the authors. The units are categorized by the two organizational types. Of these forty-three PE units, twenty-two are Type 1 and the remaining twenty-one are Type 2. As the NCSL study (2001, p. 5) notes, the auditor general is "typically responsible for conducting financial and compliance audits in addition to evaluation studies," and PE staffs are usually organized within a separate division from the financial compliance staff. California's state auditor, who

Table 5.1.   Types of State Legislative Evaluation Offices

Type 1. Auditor General or Legislative Auditor (22)

Alabama	Department of Examiner of Public Accounts
Alaska	Division of Legislative Audit
Arizona	Office of the Auditor General
Arkansas	Division of Legislative Audit
California	State Auditor, Bureau of State Audits
Colorado	Colorado State Auditor's Office
Georgia	Performance Audit Operations, Department of Audits
Hawaii	Office of the Auditor
Illinois	Office of the Auditor General
Kansas	Legislative Division of Post Audit
Louisiana	Office of the Legislative Auditor
Maryland	Office of Legislative Audits
Michigan	Office of the Auditor General
Minnesota	Office of the Legislative Auditor
Montana	Legislative Audit Division
Nevada	Legislative Counsel Bureau
New Hampshire	Office of Legislative Budget Assistant, Audit Division
Oregon	Oregon Audits Division, Secretary of State
Texas	State Auditor's Office
Utah	Office of the Legislative Auditor General
West Virginia	Performance Evaluation and Research Division
Wisconsin	Performance Audit Division, Wisconsin Legislative Audit Bureau

Type 2. Other Legislative Bodies Conducting Program Evaluations (21)

California	Office of the Legislative Analyst
Connecticut	Office of Program Review and Investigations
Florida	Office of Program Policy Analysis and Government Accountability
Idaho	Office of Performance Evaluations
Indiana	Office of Fiscal and Management Analysis
Iowa	Legislative Fiscal Bureau
Kentucky	Legislative Research Commission
Mississippi	Joint Legislative Committee on Performance Evaluation and Expenditure Review
Missouri	Oversight Division, Committee on Legislative Research
Nebraska	Nebraska Legislative Program Evaluation Unit
New Mexico	Legislative Finance Committee
North Carolina	Fiscal Research Division
North Dakota	North Dakota Legislative Council
Ohio	Legislative Office of Education Oversight
Pennsylvania	Legislative Budget and Finance Committee
South Carolina	Legislative Audit Council
Tennessee	Research and Education Accountability
Texas	Sunset Advisory Commission
Virginia	Joint Legislative Audit and Review Commission
Washington	Joint Legislative Audit and Review Committee
Wyoming	Legislative Service Office

Note: California and Texas have both Type 1 and Type 2 PE units.

is overseen by a legislative audit committee, is located in the executive branch. Oregon's state audit function is housed in the secretary of state's office.

Both Type 1 and Type 2 organizations attempt to base findings and recommendations on evidence using social science and audit methodologies. The approaches by necessity vary, depending on state laws and institutional customs, particularly when such organizations conduct investigations. The organizations are different from traditional governmental research institutes or other legislative staffs that rely upon information that is furnished to them, available in reference repositories, or available on-line. A distinguishing characteristic of these organizations is that they have the authority to command agency attention, conduct site inspections, and have direct access to data and employees inside examined agencies. Their new assertiveness has attracted attention from the media, interest groups, and scholars (Barrett, Greene, and Mariani, 2001). Because of their conflicts with "overtly 'political' branches of government," Ed Wheat (1991) characterizes state legislative audit and evaluation organizations as "activist auditors."

The research topics, priorities, and timelines of the PE units are established in various ways, but in most states, the legislature itself makes these decisions, either through (1) legislative directive (thirty-two units), such as statutory or appropriation proviso language; (2) governing committee decisions (twenty-seven units); or (3) requests from leadership or individual legislators (twenty-five units). The directors of just under half (eighteen) of the PE units may also initiate projects, whereas six units allow executive branch agencies to request examinations. The Arizona Office of the Auditor General uses a multi-attribute utility model to guide topic selection, which considers potential benefits to agencies with the concerns of legislative leadership and oversight committee members.

Types of Research and Utilization Strategies. Given the diverse placement and the historical development of the PE units, it can be expected that the products and types of evaluations are varied as well, and this turns out to be the case. Almost all of the PE units (forty) conduct performance audits or program evaluations of agency programs. Just under half of the PE units (eighteen) conduct investigations of agency programs or special incidents about which their legislature is concerned and also undertake policy analyses that consider the effects of public policies and alternatives to current policies. Nearly one-quarter of the offices (ten) have duties related to performance-based budgeting, such as assessing the reliability and validity of budget measures developed by state agencies and assessing agency progress on program performance outcomes. Seventeen PE units also conduct financial or compliance audits, sunset reviews, bill drafting, reviews of school districts, fiscal analyses, and other duties.

Complex Authorizing Environments

State legislatures operate in complex and sometimes volatile intergovernmental environments, interacting with state executive agencies as well as with local and national governments. Federal program and evaluation mandates have directly affected the operation of many intergovernmental programs that state legislatures oversee, but federal requirements appear to have had no significant impact on setting the work of state legislative PE units.

Within state governments, the decade of the 1990s saw the rise of the accountability movement as state leaders sought to reinvent government and do more with less. More state governments privatized (contracted with vendors in the private sector to perform) functions than ever before. Functions that were now being privatized included child protection, welfare eligibility determination, and human resource administration, along with routine support functions such as information technology and programming and maintenance services that already were commonly operated by private sector entities (Chi and Jasper, 1998). These trends also put more pressure on PE units to expand their analyses. PE units responded by becoming more proactive in making recommendations for increased efficiency and effectiveness and undertaking fiscal assessments of programs and new policy options to demonstrate the possible consequences of different legislative changes. About one-quarter of the PE units (thirteen) track the level of cost savings recommended in their studies and implemented by the legislature and state agencies.

State legislative elections are highly competitive in most states; in the South, previously Democratic-dominated legislatures have seen Republicans take control of one or more chambers. In addition to changing electoral politics, new methods and power centers have risen to influence the political environment. The numbers of citizen ballot initiatives have grown, and many of the initiatives have been enacted. Although legislators have kept the final authority over public policy, except in states where initiatives have expanded they have typically lost substantial power to interest groups, local governments, and the executive branch in setting the policy agenda. A new generation of interest groups represents people with simultaneously narrower yet more varied interests. These interest groups practice constituent mobilization through membership mailings and targeted media advertising. There is a wealth of policy information from think tanks and academic centers with an editorial viewpoint and recommendations for policy changes.

Legislative evaluators have to involve stakeholders at nearly every stage in the evaluation process, as stakeholders have most of the data, deal directly with citizen clients, or are citizen clients themselves and may have the strongest interest in and expertise about the programs. Stakeholders also have the most to lose if programs are terminated or substantially changed. Stakeholders, organized through interest groups, also want to be informed about investigations and possible policy changes that program evaluations may trigger. But the most overriding change for state legislatures that affects PE units may be term limits and short-term legislators. Such legislators have a different focus than traditional legislators in that they are issue-oriented, elected to office to achieve certain reforms, and often raise their own money. Legislative leadership, too, has less experience and institutional history. Studies show that, overall, legislatures continue to be more full-time and professionalized in terms of session length and salaries (Hamm and Moncrief, 1999). The "rise of professionalism," Rosenthal (1996, p. 117) notes, "has brought with it a marked increase in politicization," including an increase in the numbers of partisan staff hired by the legislature.

The 1990s have brought a changed role for program evaluation in state executive branch agencies. The widespread adoption of quality management efforts (Brudney, Hebert, and Wright, 1999) and performance-based budgeting suggests that program evaluation responsibilities have shifted away from separate PE units in the executive branch and toward program managers who have ongoing responsibility to track output and outcome measures.

Goals of PE Units

Eleanor Chelimsky (1994, pp. 494–495) discusses three objectives for program evaluation units (not limited to legislatures) that she believes must be achieved to be effective:

1. Integrate the unit, to the degree possible, with the larger organization housing it.
2. Produce strong studies that are recognized for their quality and that meet the information needs of the evaluation unit's customers.
3. Achieve measurable use of individual study findings somewhere within the government policy or program process.

Through our e-mail survey and telephone conversations, directors of legislative program evaluation units told us that they are steering their units to achieve these three goals but that additional goals have become prominent for legislative PE units as well. Examples include but are not limited to these additional goals:

4. Achieve legislative responsiveness while having an appropriate level of independence.
5. Communicate effectively in brief oral and written formats, and make greater use of Web sites and e-mail for cataloging and dissemination.
6. Produce more information in shorter timeframes while maintaining high quality.
7. Develop hybrid methods of descriptive and analytical work.
8. Educate legislators about agency programs and operations.

One of the major dilemmas the PE units face is balancing the independence of the office and its objective, nonpartisan staff with integrating the office's work into the highly political legislative institution. Some state PE directors believe that the independent PE unit is under review, if not attack. One PE director said,

> [We] have been forced to re-establish the need for [our] existence and have changed strategies and tactics. Newer generations of legislators have

questioned the need for independent, joint, non-partisan staff units given the tremendous increase in research available from a growing industry of think tanks, associations, academic units and consulting firms. This is compounded by increased research sophistication by legislators themselves, state agencies and traditional interest groups, and the ease of information sharing over the Internet.

Another PE director notes: "I don't ever remember having to defend our independence twenty years ago," but this perspective is not shared in all the states. Other PE directors say their units are not under attack. For example, a third PE director observes, "While we may face some unique challenges or pressures, overall, I think there has simply been an increased demand for accountability from all aspects of government, and we are not exempt from that." Yet another PE director rebuts:

> I don't think [in our state] we have had the questioning of the need for independent, non-partisan staff. I don't think the legislators see [think tank] reports as a replacement or competition for our work in that the liberals won't accept the work of the conservative think tanks, and vice versa. Our legislators still seem to want us as that independent voice, IF they can get our work in time frames that meet their needs.

Yet in the decade of the 1990s, the ordeals of independent, nonpartisan PE units in some states show that their purpose and usefulness can be questioned by the legislatures themselves. And when the legislature begins to attack, evaluation organizations that have stood apart from the legislative institution have had a harder time surviving. One example is the New York Legislative Commission on Expenditure Review (LCER), once a premier program evaluation operation in the 1970s, staffed by Ivy League Ph.D.'s and evaluation professionals. Several senior PE directors told us that the New York legislature abolished LCER in the early 1990s, in part because legislative commissioners either failed to attend legislative meetings or sent staff proxies. This led other legislators to conclude that the commission was too removed from the legislative institution and had lost its salience in the policy debates. In 1992, the California legislature abolished its highly regarded Auditor General's Office after a ballot proposition forced the legislature to cut its staff and budget, and the legislature chose to keep its partisan staff. After public uproar, in 1993 the legislature recreated the Auditor General's Office but placed it within the executive branch.

Roles of PE Unit and Staff

We can identify six roles of the legislative PE units that are central in today's changing legislative environment to maintain relevance and centrality:

- Role One: Educator of legislators and citizens on government programs
- Role Two: Supporter of legislative oversight with original, focused, and cost-saving information
- Role Three: Timely information providers
- Role Four: Proficient and technologically sophisticated evaluators
- Role Five: Clear and to-the-point communicators
- Role Six: "Protector of the Legislative Institution"

Each of these six roles is briefly discussed next and illustrated with examples from our interviews on current practices in the states.

Role One: Educator of Legislators and Citizens on Government Programs. In the opinion of some PE directors, citizens and legislators seem to have less knowledge about government than in past decades. Thus legislative PE staffs are increasingly taking on the role of educating new legislators about government programs and functions. One seasoned observer of the legislative scene told us that a major trend is

> an increasing need to educate members on how government works and the consequences of policy changes. Term limits and increased membership turnover have created a need for evaluators to educate legislators on the mechanics of government fiscal policy and operations. Once members become familiar with how programs operate, they have turned to us for options on consolidation of administrative entities, cost cutting proposals, funding formulas, and for sensitivity analysis of the consequences of funding changes. New members often enter public service with a view that government is bloated and that costs can be reduced. Then they discover that government is very complicated and quickly determine that cuts have consequences to local constituencies, particularly cuts to education, health and social services.

Role Two: Supporter of Legislative Oversight with Original and Focused Information. A second role is one that has been important since the 1970s, namely, legislative PE staff support legislative oversight and provide legislative information that is independent of data developed by executive branch agencies. However, the twist we heard from our respondents is that even in today's information-rich environment, PE staff are generating critical primary data and analyses that are unavailable elsewhere and that are designed specifically for legislative oversight decision making. A senior PE staff person commented that

> the use of the legislative [PE unit] helps to balance power between the executive and legislative branches. . . . The growing importance of this function [is illustrated] in Mississippi in light of the *Alexander* v. *Allain* lawsuit [that removed legislators serving on boards and commissions performing executive functions]. Importantly, legislative staffers gather information mostly

from sources that do not reside on the Internet, or even in computerized data banks. This type of analysis and evaluation is flatly unavailable anywhere else.

Part of this legislative oversight role can be described as an emerging "information broker" role that PE staff serve in our postmodern world of information overload. As one PE director writes:

> Even when the data [are] widely available, no one has read it to determine what it implies. . . . It takes special staff, who understand legislative mechanics, and who are dedicated to the principle that legislatures need independent information and analysis, to make the connection between data and legislative action.

Another PE director notes that legislators themselves generally are not researchers and need information developed regarding their own agencies and states.

> In many states, legislators are not very sophisticated yet in doing their own research, and even those that are [good at research] can't get good information from agencies about their programs. Also, especially in the smaller states, our legislators aren't 'wired' yet (their secretaries have computers on their desks, but legislators don't). . . . other research/think tanks/academic units/consultants out there don't necessarily give legislators information they can use (or trust!) in making decisions relating to their own states.

Role Three: Timely Information Providers. All of the eight state PE directors we contacted underscored the idea that their timeframes for conducting studies keep getting shorter and shorter. Information must be available to match the legislative cycle and to inform legislation and bill changes considered by the standing committees if PE products are to be viewed as useful. This is not a new trend, but it seems to be accelerating in importance. Studies in the 1980s and 1990s noted this factor (for example, Green, 1984; Brown, 1988; Bezruki, Mueller, and McKim, 1999).

The impact of legislative term limits on PE units has been hotly debated. In 1999, Mohan and Stutzman found that most staff believed term limits would greatly change the role of independent research units, but fewer thought these changes had yet occurred. However, our survey responses, nearly three years later, indicated that staffs do see changes attributed to term limits in current legislative attitudes toward program evaluation studies. As one PE director writes:

> Term limits seem to be constantly on the minds of our legislators and in the background of the timing of many of their decisions. Legislators want an answer NOW, because they want to do a bill THIS session, not a following session. I think they are more willing than ever to make a decision with limited data, rather than postpone a decision until there is better data.

Legislative PE units have responded to this shortened timeframe. Arizona's auditor general formed "rapid response" teams to produce reports quickly for legislative leadership or the appropriations chair. In 2001, the Arizona state legislature considered but failed to pass a bill that would have required this special team to produce its reports in thirty days. Mississippi's PEER committee staff performs expedited "legislative assistance" projects for members if the issue is not sensitive (that is, likely to question the character or competence of an official) and will not require more than a week or two of staff time. OPPAGA in Florida conducts "rapid response reviews" in thirty to sixty days for the legislative leadership and members, which is in keeping with the OPPAGA motto, "Accountability with a Sense of Urgency."

Role Four: Proficient and Technologially Sophisticated Evaluators. One constant factor for PE units is the need to retain highly qualified staff with multidisciplinary expertise and to adopt rigorous methods for study and documentation (National Conference of State Legislatures, 2001). The PE offices in Arizona, Florida, Mississippi, and Virginia have employed full-time "methodologists" who consult with teams, promote sophisticated approaches, and work collaboratively with statisticians working for stakeholders who stand ready to challenge the validity of any weak methodologies. In 1984, a Tennessee PE director working for the legislature (Funkhouser, 1984, p. 261), wrote:

> The arena within which we operate tends to push us toward methodological rigor because that protects us against error. In many of the states our work is very adversarial. . . . Because it is an adversarial environment and because our opponents possess far greater resources than we do, we can be virtually assured that if we make an embarrassing error, it will be found and exposed.

To promote consistent and professional work standards, the NCSL study (2001) found that the majority of PE units have formally adopted professional standards to guide their work, whereas other offices rely on them in less formal ways.

Today's legislative PE staffs conduct a wide range of evaluation studies, from formative and process studies in the early phases of program implementation to outcome and assessment studies as programs mature. Both qualitative methods (for example, focus groups, in-depth interviews, and site visits) as well as quantitative methods (for example, econometric models, parametric and nonparametric statistical analysis, and geographic information systems) are used, whereas hybrid approaches have become more the norm than previously. Justification reviews, analysis of policy alternatives and their consequences (such as new funding formulas), and cost-savings assessments have become more widely used in the 1990s. Policy analysis studies are also examining broader, more sensitive issues using newer approaches that delve into areas heretofore considered the realm of professionally licensed or accredited experts. For example, Virginia's JLARC has recently used "value analysis" in a study of capital punishment that included examining stakeholder values and highly sensitive prosecutor records.

Legislative evaluators have fully integrated technology into their work. Nearly all evaluators do their own typing and use desktop computers for importing external data and preparing spreadsheets, charts, and electronic presentations. Evaluators are using geographic information systems (GISs) for mapping government services by district, statistical software packages to analyze large sets of data, electronic surveys to simplify response and improve accuracy of data compilation, as well as computer listservs to send out summary information to citizens and legislators.

Role Five: Clear and to-the-Point Communicators. All the PE directors noted the importance of good communication for their work to have maximum impact. One PE director expressed the following colorful summary:

> We definitely have had to build strengths in communications, because (1) legislators are overwhelmed with information, and (2) more and more legislators grew up watching TV to get most of their news. When I see the stacks of papers, reports, letters on legislators' desks I feel like the Seven Up delivery man fighting for shelf space for his product in the supermarket with the big brands like Pepsi, and Coca Cola. I know I'm going to get one shot to get their attention, and the time they are giving to my report during that one shot is limited. If it isn't easy to read and interesting, forget it. We're a generation raised on sound bytes and we have adapted our delivery to that fact.

PE units prefer to find a report format and writing style the legislature is comfortable with and then to stick with that strategy. Legislators appreciate this because they do not have time to search through reports looking for "bottom lines" or recommendations. Common formats include a free-standing executive summary for longer reports, color graphics, and "meaningful" captions that are written to facilitate scanning by busy readers. Most of the reports by OPPAGA in Florida are in a two-column newsletter format and are fewer than twenty pages long, whereas "Justification Reviews" or major examinations follow a traditional report format. PE units in Minnesota and Virginia write longer and more detailed reports. The writing styles of most organizations stress use of the active voice and making points up front, followed by sufficient explanation and illustration.

Role Six: "Protector of the Legislative Institution." Finally, across the country legislative PE staff note the increased competition, partisanship, and tensions within state legislatures; some believe that the nonpartisan research staff are playing a broader role in helping legislatures find their balance. One of the PE directors helped define the sixth role of PE units—"protector of the institution"—by asserting:

There is another very subtle role of "protector of the institution." Having the ability to turn to a respected, nonpartisan research arm as a touchstone in times of "gridlock" is an important institutional capacity. In addition, evaluation staffs are used as a key tool when the primary interest is descriptive (e.g., What is this program and how does it work?) or policy related (e.g., What are our options in this particularly sticky situation?). These two observations may simply reflect the fact that, after some 30 years, legislative evaluation has found its niche in the broader legislative arena and is being used to find the common ground and serve as a starting point for dialogue on controversial issues.

Conclusion

Legislative evaluation has evolved and adapted to the pressures of the exploding information age at the beginning of the twenty-first century. The diverse roles that legislative program evaluation offices fill today are affected by internal state environmental forces—a major one being term limits—resulting in shortened timeframes for conducting evaluation and changes in how legislators set the priorities for their terms in office. This is reflective of a larger paradigm shift in these evaluation units, as legislative program evaluation offices are no longer simply nonpartisan program evaluation staff who work independently from legislators and whose work remains largely unaffected by the political gamesmanship that takes place in the legislative arena. Rather, the new paradigm is one in which evaluation offices are integrated with other legislative research units, work closely with legislators, and increasingly compete with partisan staff and an abundance of think tanks for the attention of decision makers. Yet the evaluation offices often are highly respected and relied upon by legislators for competent analysis of the tough policy and fiscal issues they must address.

Although some PE directors feel that this new paradigm has resulted in an increased need to justify their existence, others feel that it suggests that the work is viewed as more vital than ever, serving to provide guidance through the increasing information overload experienced by legislators. Regardless of these differing experiences, the fact remains that state legislative program evaluation offices have proven to be organic units. How these offices have responded to the increasingly partisan legislatures and competitive environment differs among states and appears largely dependent on internal state factors. What these specific factors are remain difficult to generalize. However, this chapter has taken a step forward by framing the new paradigm of legislative program evaluation and offering an overview of the newer goals and roles that program evaluation units play as a result of the authorizing environment within which they work.

Note

1. The so-called Yellow Book published by the Comptroller General of the United States (1994, p. 14) defines *performance auditing* as "an objective and systematic

examination of evidence for the purpose of providing an independent assessment of the performance of a government organization, program activity, or function in order to provide information to improve public accountability and facilitate decision-making by parties with responsibility to oversee or initiate corrective actions."

References

Barrett, K., Greene, R., and Mariani, M. "Managing for Results: Grading the States." *Governing,* 2001, *14*(5), 42, 48,58,71,74,90,98,102. Accessible at governing.com/gpp/gp1intro.htm.

Berry, F., and Flowers, G. "Public Entrepreneurs in the Policy Process: Performance-based Budgeting Reform in Florida." *Journal of Public Budgeting, Accounting and Financial Management,* 1999, *11*(4), 578–617.

Bezruki, D., Mueller, J., and McKim, K. "Legislative Utilization of Evaluations." In R. K. Jonas (ed.), *Legislative Program Evaluation: Utilization-Driven Research for Decision Makers.* New Directions for Evaluation, no. 81. San Francisco: Jossey-Bass, 1999.

Brooks, R. "Blending Two Cultures: State Legislative Auditing and Evaluation." In C. Wisler (ed.), *Evaluation and Auditing: Prospects for Convergence,* New Directions for Evaluation, no. 71. San Francisco: Jossey-Bass, 1996.

Brown, J. "State Evaluation in a Legislative Environment: Adapting Evaluation to Legislative Needs." In C. Wye and H. Hatry, (eds.), *Timely, Low-Cost Evaluation in the Public Sector,* New Directions for Program Evaluation, no. 38. San Francisco: Jossey-Bass, 1988.

Brudney, J., Hebert, T., and Wright, D. "Reinventing Government in the American States: Measuring and Explaining Administrative Reform." *Public Administration Review,* 1999, *59*(1), 19–30.

Chelimsky, E. "Making Evaluation Units Effective." In J. Wholey, H. Hatry, and K. Newcomer (eds.), *Handbook of Program Evaluation,* San Francisco: Jossey-Bass, 1994.

Chi, K., and Jasper, C. *Private Practices: A Review of Privatization in State Government.* Lexington, Ky.: Council of State Governments, 1998.

Comptroller General of the United States. *Government Auditing Standards.* Washington D.C.: U.S. General Accounting Office, 1994.

Crane, E. "Legislative Services Agencies." In R. Weber and R. Marcelli (eds.), *Book of the States 1972–73.* Lexington, Ky.: Council of State Governments, 1972.

Felbinger, C. "The Process of Evaluation." R. Bingham and C. Felbinger (eds.), *Evaluation in Practice: A Methodological Approach.* New York: Longman, 1989.

Funkhouser, M. "Current Issues in Legislative Program Evaluation." *Public Administration Review,* 1984, *44*(3), 261–263.

Gray, V., and Lowery, D. "Interest Representation in the States." In R. Weber and P. Brace (eds.), *American State and Local Politics.* New York: Chatham House, 1999.

Green, A. "The Role of Evaluation in Legislative Decision Making." *Public Administration Review,* 1984, *44*(3), 265–267.

Hamm, K., and Moncrief, G. "Legislative Politics in the States." In V. Gray, R. Hanson, and H. Jacob, (eds.), *Politics in the American States: A Comparative Analysis.* Washington D.C.: Congressional Quarterly Press, 1999, 144–190.

Melkers, J., and Willoughby, K. "The State of the States: Performance-based Budgeting Requirements in 47 out of 50." *Public Administration Review,* 1998, *58*(1), 66–73.

Mohan, R., and Stutzman, M. "The Impact of Term Limits on Legislative Program Evaluation." In R. K. Jonas (ed.), *Legislative Program Evaluation: Utilization-Driven Research for Decision Makers.* New Directions for Evaluation, no. 81. San Francisco: Jossey-Bass, 1999.

National Academy of Public Administration. *A Government to Trust and Respect: Rebuilding Citizen-Government Relations for the 21st Century.* Washington, D.C.: National Academy of Public Administration, 1999.

National Conference of State Legislatures (NCSL). *Ensuring the Public Trust: How Program Policy Evaluation Serves State Legislatures.* Denver: National Conference of State Legislatures, 2001. Accessible at www.ncsl.org/programs/nlpes.

National Legislative Program Evaluation Society (NLPES). *Topic Selection Practices: What Useful Practices Have Your Staff or Oversight Committee Adopted to Help Identify the Projects Your Office Should Undertake?* Survey accessible only at www.ncsl.org/programs/nlpes/survey.htm#selectionpractices. June-July, 2001.

Rosenthal, A. "The Legislature: Unraveling of Institutional Fabric." C. Van Horn (ed.), *The State of the States.* Washington, D.C.: Congressional Quarterly Press, 1996.

Wheat, E. "Reinventing Performance Auditing." *National Association of Local Government Auditors Quarterly,* Dec. 1991. Accessible at www.nalga.org/qrhy/12.9313.html.

FRANCES S. BERRY *is professor and master's of public administration director at the Askew School of Public Administration and Policy at Florida State University, Tallahassee.*

JOHN W. TURCOTTE *is director of the Florida legislature's Office of Program Policy Analysis and Government Accountability, Tallahassee.*

SARAH C. LATHAM *is policy director for the Florida legislature's Council for Education Policy, Research and Improvement, Tallahassee.*

6

The editors make note of several trends and implications arising from the discussions in the earlier chapters, in particular, the need to recognize the complexity of evaluation contexts involving multiple sponsors and stakeholders. The significance of the multifaceted and complex environment for the conduct of evaluation in state and local government settings is noted, a summary of the historical context is provided, and a discussion of the importance of maintaining evaluator independence and objectivity when addressing the diverse needs of sponsors and stakeholders is included.

Addressing Sponsor and Stakeholder Needs in the Evaluation Authorizing Environment: Trends and Implications

David J. Bernstein, Maria D. Whitsett, Rakesh Mohan

In the Editors' Notes of this volume, we suggest that one challenge facing evaluators working in state and local government settings, either as evaluation staff, consultants, or nonprofit service providers, is to adapt to the needs and requirements of various stakeholders. We suggest that individuals who have an interest in an evaluation, including the organizations that sponsor evaluation research through funding and legal authorization, have divergent priorities and interests. It therefore would be prudent to understand the sociopolitical environment in which evaluators operate, or what we refer to more broadly as the "evaluation authorizing environment." Further, we suggest that meeting the needs of diverse stakeholders, given fiscal, political, and logistical challenges, tests the professional skills of evaluators. The viability of evaluation professionals and the evaluation profession can be, in part, determined by the ability of evaluators to provide high-level, objective evaluation services in such a complex and demanding environment. The chapters in this volume provide a variety of useful and thought-provoking examples with which to explore this conceptualization.

The views expressed in this chapter are the authors' and do not necessarily represent those of Montgomery County, Maryland, the Austin Independent School District, Texas, or the Washington State Joint Legislative Audit and Review Committee.

Authorizing Environment: Historical Context

Fredericks, Carman, and Birkland set the stage by exploring the historical, political, and institutional factors affecting evaluation in state and local settings. In particular, Fredericks and her colleagues summarize four interrelated trends that have given social service providers an opportunity to expand their role, thus entering these organizations into the remarkably challenging and complex environment that is the subject of this volume, including

*   The increased interest in accountability and performance measurement in all levels of government and in the nonprofit sector
*   The devolution of social services from the federal level to states
*   The increased reliance on nonprofit organizations for service delivery
*   The proliferation of complex social service provider networks made up of multiple sponsors and stakeholders

Managing for Performance and Outcomes. One of the more obvious trends in state and local evaluation is the increased interest in accountability and performance measurement, which is attributable both directly and indirectly to the legislative requirements imposed on federal agencies by the Government Performance and Results Act (GPRA) of 1993 (107 State. 285, PL 103–62, 1993). The vast number of federally funded services offered by local governments, using funds passed through state authorizing and allocation processes, meant it was only a question of time until the federal infrastructure would require reporting on outcomes, even though GPRA contained no specific provision requiring local governments to produce such data.

Heightened attention to outcomes is not always received sympathetically by local governments, which are then forced to find a way to shape evaluations to meet local needs in addition to fulfilling externally imposed requirements related to outcomes. We see this played out in Boser's discussion of the Even Start program, with issues similar to those driving local evaluation efforts in the California state authorizing environment, as described in Tang and others and Guzmán and Feria. Despite the focus on outcomes from higher levels of what Guzmán and Feria call the "hierarchy of key stakeholders," local evaluations typically focus on program improvement rather than a demonstration of outcomes that may or may not capture the priorities and goals of local authorities. The greatest possible tension and disagreement may arise when the outcomes that local authorities must demonstrate are perceived as either having no bearing on, or as being incompatible with, the locally defined priorities.

The direct impact of GPRA on state and local governments has been accompanied by an indirect impact, with increased emphasis on the results of programs by authorizing organizations. The emphasis on outcomes that

Birkland and colleagues note has created some backlash. Direct service providers resist the concept of being graded, whether that is done on the basis of outside assessments of the value of services or comparisons to other entities with whom the subject organization may or may not be comparable. Program sponsors tend to be more interested in evaluation results that focus on program improvement and process, whereas outside parties appear to be more interested in outcomes. There is even some disagreement about whether the focus on outcomes truly captures the most meaningful program impact, with at least one author (Boser) questioning outside assessments and whether they are in fact "real," that is, sensitive to the most meaningful program outcomes. Designs must be sensitive to program improvements and outcomes, which may be possible if local governments are permitted to focus evaluation activities on their areas of interest.

Devolution and Enhanced Opportunities for Complex Networks of Nonprofit Social Service Providers. Fredericks, Carman, and Birkland discuss the historical trend of devolution of services from the federal sector to the state and local sector; they correctly point out that limited service capacity at the local level to handle these new responsibilities has resulted in nonprofit organizations assuming a larger role for publicly sponsored social service programs. Given the number of social service programs and the continued interest of state government, local government agencies, and service-specific interest groups, a complex network of service providers with both formal and informal modes of interaction has developed. In the case of a national program such as Even Start, which Boser discusses, this web of interested stakeholders becomes a truly complex national network. Even in the case of a single state initiative such as the Tobacco Control Program (TCP) that Tang and others discuss, the wide variety of program stakeholders and community interests poses a complex series of challenges in efforts to design evaluations that encompass varied interests and data needs.

Other Challenges. Fredericks and her colleagues identify four additional trends as evidence of the complex authorizing environment:

• Variation in the capacity and commitment to evaluation
• The presence and interests of multiple stakeholders
• Staff and managerial commitment
• Fears about cross-site comparisons and being graded

Each of these issues is discussed, in whole or in part, in the chapters by Boser, Tang, and others, and by Guzmán and Feria. In particular, the capacity and interest of local or community-based organizations (CBOs) to meet the complex and often divergent evaluative needs of different stakeholders, while still providing useful information to local managers and stakeholders interested in program improvement, is a unifying theme of these chapters. Evaluators are challenged to conduct evaluations in complex multistakeholder environments, given

- Diverse interests of stakeholders
- Varying degrees of direct and indirect power to influence conduct of an evaluation
- Differences of opinion about the primary focus and need for evaluation information
- Limited resources and potentially limited evaluative capacity of local evaluators
- Resistance to evaluation from program management and staff
- Pressure to put funding for direct services first

The presence and interests of multiple stakeholders is a recurrent theme in every chapter, reflecting the decision to incorporate them into a single volume of *New Directions*. In addition to the federal and state authorizing entities and local service providers discussed in the Boser, Tang, and others, and Guzmán and Feria chapters, Berry and colleagues identify another historical development affecting a critical stakeholder in the state and local government evaluation authorizing environment: the state legislature. Although being required to fund federally mandated evaluation activities, state legislatures operate in a highly politicized environment, with state legislative program evaluation staff being put in the position of trying to meet the wide variety of interests of individual legislators. Berry and colleagues identify historical trends that are affecting the nature and focus of activities by professional, nonpartisan staff who serve the evaluation and information needs of state legislators. These trends, including term limits, the professionalization of legislatures, the issue-orientation of term-limited legislators, and the changes affecting the legislative evaluation function, set the context for understanding the complexities of state-funded evaluation activities in the multistakeholder environment.

Finally, several chapters discuss fears about cross-site comparisons and resistance to the concept of being graded, with the constant threat of losing funding if programs are not favorably evaluated. Local programs thus may resist outcome evaluation imposed by outside authorizing organizations because they perceive they are being judged or graded on criteria and outcomes that they do not believe fairly represent their programmatic realities and that may threaten the livelihood of programs in which they are personally invested. Boser also notes that many local governments view federal data gathering with some resistance, seeing it as ill-suited for accurately capturing what they consider to be the "real" outcomes of their program, yet at the same time grading or judging their work in ways that could adversely affect their funding.

Potential Strategies for Coping with Complex Authorizing Environments

Despite the complex challenges that face state and local government evaluators in the multistakeholder, multi-interest evaluation environment, each of the chapters identifies what we will call "coping strategies." Coping strategies seek to encourage the best use of evaluation activities in order to meet the varying needs of stakeholders. Although win-win situations may not always be possible, these coping strategies provide state and local government evaluators with options to address the wide variety of needs of authorizing organizations and stakeholders.

Fredericks, Carman, and Birkland cite the benefits of performing network analysis to understand the relationships and interests of various stakeholders. This analysis would examine the formal and informal structures in the program and the nature and density of linkages between stakeholders. The authors also stress the importance of building an evaluation culture in which all members of an organization are committed to the purposes and goals of evaluation projects. In particular, they indicate that it is critical to get management's active commitment to the evaluation. One cannot help but wonder if, in the contemporary world of program evaluation, network analysis should become a core component of evaluability and feasibility assessments.

Although not directly saying so, Fredericks and colleagues, and to a greater extent the chapters that follow, demonstrate the value of using a variety of evaluation methodologies to meet varying stakeholder needs. This is most evident in the chapter by Tang and others, where use of empowerment evaluation and case studies was combined with state-mandated efforts to collect standardized outcome data. The capacity to use multiple methods to meet a variety of evaluation needs clearly points to a need for extensive training in evaluation methods for professional evaluators so that they can acquire the variety of skills and approaches needed to simultaneously accommodate so many divergent interests. In other words, evaluators in the complex authorizing environments described in this volume must have extensive and sophisticated repertoires to experience a modicum of success.

Fredericks and colleagues identify two ways to deal with fears of being graded. They indicate the importance of explaining what evaluation is, why it is being conducted, and how evaluation can contribute to local management, service delivery, and better outcomes; they equally emphasize the importance of communicating what evaluation is not. The importance of communication in the processes of planning and conducting evaluations involving multiple stakeholders is paramount to building positive evaluation cultures within and among stakeholders.

Similarly to Fredericks and colleagues, Guzmán and Feria stress the value of identifying critical stakeholders and of communication in meeting state-mandated evaluation policies. They emphasize the importance of constant negotiations with various stakeholders, including the sponsor (for example, the state), various critical local stakeholders, and indirect stakeholders who have the potential to influence program implementation and evaluation, even if not directly involved in program implementation. The hierarchy of stakeholders provides a useful understanding of the political realities involved in gaining and maintaining access to carry out evaluation activities and is similar to the suggestion by Fredericks and her colleagues that network analysis can be a component of evaluation planning. Thus failure to attend to the full complexity of relationships in the authorizing environment is likely to be associated with, at best, unnecessary difficulty in completing an adequate evaluation and, at worst, complete derailment of the evaluation.

From Guzmán and Feria's point of view, no amount of planning is more important than the need for evaluators to be flexible. They argue that flexibility in implementation of evaluation designs is seen as a practical reality and a benefit, not a threat to the validity of evaluations. Some would question their suggestion that the evaluation plan should *always* be subject to revision and that such revisions would, in fact, enhance rather than detract from the validity of an evaluation. These doubts aside, the reality of implementation issues and the need to be considerate of stakeholder issues of timing are important considerations that should be included in an evaluation plan so that realistic deadlines can be established. As Guzmán and Feria indicate, the needs of the stakeholders, the broader community, and the target population are continuously being shaped and adjusted by contextual factors. The chapter serves as a reminder of how important it is to keep stakeholders informed and to protect access to evaluation subjects, as an evaluation design is meaningless without the ability to have access to subjects who are the basis of intervention and evaluation activities.

Boser documents an interesting approach to meeting the needs of various stakeholders. In addition to requiring national evaluation studies, the federal legislation authorizing Even Start required that each project conduct a local evaluation (PL 103–382, Sec. 1205) with the explicit goal of providing information to local stakeholders for program improvement (U.S. Department of Education, 1998). Some states dictated the focus of the local evaluation component, whereas others provided localities with the flexibility to meet their own needs. In the complex authorizing environment of a major federally funded program, this legislatively mandated model demonstrates a creative way to address the needs of federal policymakers for documentation of outcomes, state policymakers for documentation of accountability, and local government for documentation of methods to improve programs and processes. This flexibility provides an opportunity for local governments to focus on issues of importance to them rather than to focus exclusively on, as Boser says, "an experimental design for the in depth study [that] fails to capture evidence of stronger impact because it removes the contextual elements." Most important, local case studies helped build local support for and ownership of the program being evaluated, which is critical to success in a complex intergovernmental process.

Tang and colleagues found that sponsoring agencies can derive many benefits from providing technical assistance to service providers and local authorities. Such benefits include enhancing a thorough and mutual understanding of the needs of the agencies involved, increasing trust, and empowering the affected agency to maximize the value of its required participation in an evaluation, while simultaneously promoting improved performance in terms of both implementation and results. Technical assistance in the evaluation of the California TBC took the form of state-produced documents to provide information about the value and conduct of evaluation, as well as one-on-one technical support from a contract evaluation consultant. This allowed the program to collect information that it needed to demonstrate outcomes, while providing local programs the opportunity to collect information of interest, thus encouraging a sense of local control and influence. The methodological shift recognized what Tang and colleagues consider the serious limitations of a traditional evaluation that employs an independent researcher to evaluate hundreds of local programs. They found latter stages of the TCP evaluation more useful than earlier ones, in that they enhanced local capacity, provided standardized information to the state, and allowed local programs a sense of self-control while affording them an opportunity to improve program management and results.

Berry and her colleagues identify three critical trends in legislative program evaluation that serve to both challenge responsive evaluators and potentially provide coping mechanisms for meeting stakeholder needs and opportunities for growth of the evaluation field. First, they discuss the increasing professionalization of state legislatures and the narrow interest-specific orientation of some legislators. Although this makes the process of meeting any given legislator's evaluation needs more challenging, it also provides a more sophisticated and arguably a more interested audience for evaluation products. Second, the increased interest in, and in many cases the legislative mandate for, performance-based budgets (Melkers and Willoughby, 1998) provides another opportunity for evaluators to use their unique skills to positively influence the correct use of performance measures to support evaluation activities (Bernstein, 1999). Third, the professionalization of state legislative program evaluation staff, despite increased politicization of the evaluation environment, permits demonstration of the positive contribution that professional evaluators can make in society.

Evaluator Independence, Objectivity, Integrity, Credibility, and Cooperation

It is clear that successfully dealing with the complex network of evaluation sponsors and stakeholders may, at times, compromise an evaluator's appearance as independent and objective. As noted by Berry, Turcotte, and Latham, according to legislative evaluation directors, one of the prominent goals for a legislative evaluation unit, as identified by legislative evaluation directors, is to achieve legislative responsiveness while having an appropriate level of independence. Some may question the importance, or even the reality of "objectivity." Be that as it may, many evaluators, particularly those trained as auditors, and many evaluation clients may feel that an evaluator's work is strengthened when the evaluator maintains an objective perspective, is seen by others as being independent and objective, and when the evaluator's interaction with sponsors and stakeholders does not compromise his or her independence. To many, the credibility of evaluation work is indeed dependent on the maintenance of this appearance of independence and objectivity.

Federal auditors, as well as many state and local government auditors, are obligated to follow generally accepted government auditing standards, known more informally by the acronym GAGAS, or the Yellow Book standards, named for the yellow cover of the U.S. General Accounting Office publication that contains these standards (Comptroller General of the United States, 1994). Three sections of the Yellow Book specifically relate to auditor independence. Section 3.11 states that audit organizations and the individual auditors should be free from impairments to independence, should be organizationally independent, and should maintain an independent attitude and appearance. Section 3.13 states that auditors should consider whether their attitudes and beliefs will affect their independence and also whether there is anything about their situations that might lead others to question their independence. Section 3.12 places the responsibility on both the auditor and the audit organization for maintaining independence so that the audit findings, conclusions, and recommendations can be viewed as impartial. Auditors working in audit units that require following these standards likely would be compelled to observe these standards, regardless of whether the work being performed is purely audit-related or could be broadly seen as encompassing evaluation work.

Like the Yellow Book, the Program Evaluation Standards established by the Joint Committee on Standards for Educational Evaluation in 1994 also recognize the challenge of addressing and balancing the competing needs of evaluation sponsors and stakeholders. Two complementary statements of the Program Evaluation Standards, U2 and P7, address evaluator credibility and conflict of interest (Joint Committee on Standards for Educational Evaluation, 1994). Statement U2 requires evaluators to "be both trustworthy and competent to perform the evaluation, so that the evaluation findings achieve maximum credibility and acceptance." Statement P7 adds that "conflict of interest should be dealt with openly and honestly, so that it does not compromise the evaluation processes and results."

The American Evaluation Association (AEA) Guiding Principles for Evaluators also provide insight on how evaluators can be expected to act when dealing with sponsors and stakeholders. As indicated on the AEA Web site, the Guiding Principles "were developed to guide the professional practice of evaluators, and inform evaluation clients and the general public about the principles they can expect to be upheld by professional evaluators" (American Evaluation Association, 2002). The Guiding Principles, in fact, demonstrate considerable sensitivity to the issues that are the focus of this volume. Three of the five principles are particularly relevant: (1)

ensuring integrity and honesty, (2) respecting people, and (3) considering the general and public welfare.

Guiding Principle Three encourages evaluators to be sensitive to the honesty and integrity of the entire evaluation process. As with the Yellow Book Standards and the Program Evaluation Standards discussed earlier, the honesty and integrity of the evaluation process and the evaluator can bolster the credibility of the process. Honesty and integrity in dealing with sponsors and stakeholders will build credibility with them and may address the fear of being evaluated or graded that was mentioned earlier in this volume.

Statement C4, intended to illustrate Guiding Principle Three, discusses the need for evaluators to disclose potential conflicts of interest. Statement C3 indicates that evaluator, client, and stakeholder interests should be explicated. An honest airing of these interests, and potential conflicts of interest, can improve acceptance of the evaluation process and results. Additionally, a forthright disclosure of such interests can help to ensure understanding of contextual factors, acceptance of evaluation findings, and use of evaluation results. As such, it is a highly valuable coping strategy for dealing with the complexities of responding to sponsor and stakeholder needs.

Guiding Principle Four addresses the need for respect for people and for ensuring the dignity and self-worth of all parties involved in the evaluation process. Maintaining a focus on respect for both sponsors and stakeholders and ensuring understanding among all parties of the complexities involved in these relationships will further the usefulness of the evaluation process. Mutual respect should also promote acceptance by some, if not most, parties regarding the conduct of the evaluation and the role of the evaluator.

Finally, Guiding Principal Five addresses the need to articulate and take into account the diversity of interests and values that may be related to the general and public welfare. Statement E4 specifically addresses an almost universal tension that exists between the interest of an evaluation client, whom we have been referring to as the evaluation sponsor, and other interests and needs. Statement E4 recognizes the need to meet client needs whenever feasible and appropriate. At the same time, E4 implies the potential conflict between client and stakeholder needs that was made evident in this volume's chapters. Statement E4 points out that client needs may conflict with systematic inquiry, competence, integrity, and respect for people that are the focus of the first four Guiding Principles. Statement E4 also provides a suggested process for addressing such conflicts, wherein, "evaluators should explicitly identify and discuss the conflicts with the client and relevant stakeholders, resolve them when possible, determine whether continued work on the evaluation is advisable if the conflicts cannot be resolved, and make clear any significant limitations on the evaluation that might result if the conflict is not resolved" (American Evaluation Association, 2002).

An approach such as this suggests a useful and pragmatic solution to addressing the inherent conflicts in wanting to meet client needs, being sensitive to stakeholder issues, ensuring the integrity and value of the evaluation process, and attempting to address the complexities of dealing with the complex evaluation authorizing environment. As can be seen from the preceding discussion, the three sets of standards remind evaluators that independence and objectivity are useful attributes in effectively conducting evaluations and can help educate sponsors and stakeholders on the nature of sound evaluation practices. As such, the credibility and effectiveness of evaluation, evaluators, and the evaluation profession are enhanced.

Conclusion

This volume shows that the state and local government evaluation context, or authorizing environment, even though complex and multifaceted, provides a wealth of opportunities for evaluators to demonstrate professionalism and commitment in the face of significant professional, economic, and political threats. We are optimistic that the future will bring expanded use of evaluation to meet the diverse needs of sponsors and stakeholders. Evaluators will be offered opportunities for career growth and development, while the evaluation field can continue to foster and encourage social good by providing high-quality, useful information to improve program efficiency, effectiveness, and equity as it meets the needs of diverse stakeholders and sponsors in the state and local government evaluation authorizing environment.

References

American Evaluation Association. "Guiding Principles for Evaluators." In W. R. Shadish, D. L. Newman, M. A. Scheirer, and C. Wye (eds.), *Guiding Principles for Evaluators*, New Directions for Program Evaluation, no. 66. San Francisco: Jossey-Bass. 2002. Accessible at eval.org/EvaluationDocuments/aeaprin6.html.

Bernstein, D. J. "In Response: Comments on Perrin's 'Effective Use and Misuse of Performance Measurement.'" *American Journal of Evaluation*, 1999, 20(1), 85–93.

Comptroller General of the United States. *Government Auditing Standards.* (rev. ed.) Washington, D.C.: U.S. General Accounting Office, 1994.

Joint Committee on Standards for Educational Evaluation. *Program Evaluation Standards.* Thousand Oaks, Calif.: Sage, 1994.

Melkers, J., and Willoughby, K. "The State of the States: Performance-Based Budgeting Requirements in 47 out of 50." *Public Administration Review*, 1998, 58(1), 66–73.

U.S. Department of Education. *Even Start: Evidence from the Past and a Look to the Future* Washington, D.C.: U.S. Department of Education, Planning and Evaluation Services, 1998.

DAVID J. BERNSTEIN is administrative coordinator for the Montgomery County, Maryland, Department of Finance. He is former chair of the State and Local Government Topical Interest Group of the AEA, a member of the board of directors of the American Society for Public Administration Center for Accountability and Performance, and adjunct professor of public administration at The George Washington University.

MARIA D. WHITSETT is chief accountability officer for the Austin Independent School District, Texas. She is former chair of the State and Local Government Topical Interest Group and is current chair of the PreK–12 Educational Evaluation Topical Interest Group of the AEA.

RAKESH MOHAN is a staff member of the Washington State Joint Legislative Audit and Review Committee. He is the current chair of the State and Local Government Topical Interest Group of the AEA.

INDEX

Krackhardt, D., 13, 15
Kubisch, A. C., 9

Lambert, F. C., 11
Latham, S. C., 73
Layzer, J. I., 24, 26, 30
Lester, J. P., 2, 15
Levine, M., 61, 68
Leviton, L. C., 40
Lincoln, Y., 31
Lipsky, M., 8, 9
Lipsey, M. W., 5, 40
Local program evaluation, 39–55, 94; decentralization of, 53; and empowerment evaluation, 39–41; evaluators' assertive stance in, 35; and federal directives and data gathering, 23, 92; intended aim of, 34; of national program, 26–27; and policy agenda, 23; program improvement focus of, 90; and public policy formulation, 2. *See also* California's Tobacco Control Program (TCP)
Lowery, D., 74

Macffree, K., 60
Malarcher, A. M., 41
Management information systems (MISs), 11
Managers, project commitment of, 12, 16–17
Mariani, M., 78
Martin, L. J., 5
Maxwell, C. M., 23
Mazmanian, D., 14
McKim, K., 83
McMullan, B. J., 6, 17
Measurement constructs, and cultural variation among participants, 27–28
Media Tracking Study, 42–43
Medicaid, 7, 8
Melkers, J., 75, 95
Methodology: in Even Start evaluations, 27–30; mixed-method, 35; variety in, 93
Mississippi Joint Legislative Committee on Performance Evaluation and Expenditure Review (PEER), 76
Mohan, R., 83, 89
Moncrief, G., 79
Morely, E., 6
Morrow, L. M., 23

Mueller, J., 83
Murray, S., 26

Nash, J. K., 60
Nathan, R. P., 7
National Academy of Public Administration, 74
National Conference of State Legislatures (NCSL), 73, 76, 84
National evaluations, and federal policymaking context, 34
National Legislative Program Evaluation Society (NLPES), 76; professional evaluation standards of, 76
National Performance Review, 6
National program evaluation, 25–30, 34
Neighborhood Youth Corps, 8
Network analysis, 15–16, 93, 94
Neuman, S., 31, 33
New York Legislative Commission on Expenditure Review (LCER), 73, 81
New York State Even Start Family Literacy Partnership, 25, 30–34; evaluation lessons learned from, 33–34; and local support and ownership, 33–34; longitudinal evaluation study of, 31–34
Nickse, R. A., 34
Nixon administration, 7
Nonprofit organizations: outcome measures and, 6; as public service providers, 6, 8–9

Oliver, C., 12
Online Tobacco Information System (OTIS), 47–50, 52
Osborne, D. E., 6, 11
O'Toole, L. J., Jr., 15
Outcomes: emphasis on, 90–91; government reinvention and, 6. *See* Performance measures
Owen, J. M., 11

Page, D. J., 16
Palumbo, D. J., 2
Patrizi, P., 6, 17
Patton, M. Q., 5, 17, 57
Performance audits, 75
Performance-based budgeting, 75, 78, 80; and correct use of performance measures, 95
Perkins, D. V., 61, 68

Back Issue/Subscription Order Form

Copy or detach and send to:
Jossey-Bass, 989 Market Street, San Francisco CA 94103-1741

Call or fax toll free!
Phone 888-378-2537 6AM-5PM PST; Fax 888-481-2665

Back issues: Please send me the following issues at $27 each.
(Important: please include series initials and issue number, such as EV77.)

1. EV _____

_____

_____

$ _____ Total for single issues

$ _____ SHIPPING CHARGES:

	SURFACE	Domestic	Canadian
First Item		$5.00	$6.00
Each Add'l Item		$3.00	$1.50

For next-day and second-day delivery rates, call the number listed above.

Subscriptions   Please ❏ start ❏ renew my subscription to *New Directions for Evaluation* for the year ___ at the following rate:

U.S.	❏ Individual $69	❏ Institutional $145
Canada	❏ Individual $69	❏ Institutional $185
All Others	❏ Individual $93	❏ Institutional $219

$ _____ Total single issues and subscriptions (Add appropriate sales tax for your state for single issue orders. No sales tax for U.S. subscriptions.Canadian residents, add GST for subscriptions and single issues.)

❏ Payment enclosed (U.S. check or money order only.)

❏ VISA, MC, AmEx, Discover Card #_____ Exp. date_____

Signature _____ Day phone _____

❏ Bill me (U.S. institutional orders only. Purchase order required.)

Purchase order #_____

Name _____

Address _____

_____

Phone_____ E-mail _____

For more information about Jossey-Bass, visit our Web site at:
www.josseybass.com   **PRIORITY CODE = ND1**